D1637103

Hunting Trophy Muskies & Northerns

Hunting Trophy Muskies & Northerns

Complete Angler's Library™
North American Fishing Club
Minneapolis, Minnesota

Hunting Trophy
Muskies & Northerns

Library of Congress Catalog Card Number 92-80358
ISBN 0-914697-45-5

Printed in U.S.A.
      3   4   5   6   7   8   9

The North American Fishing Club
offers a line of hats for fishermen.
For information, write:
      North American Fishing Club
      P.O. Box 3403
      Minnetonka, MN 55343

Contents

Acknowledgments

The North American Fishing Club would like to thank all those who have helped make this book a reality.

Wildlife artist Virgil Beck created the cover art. Artist David Rottinghaus provided all illustrations. Photos, in addition to the authors', were provided by Harold Anderson, Paul DeMarchi, Doug Stange, Marc Wisniewski/Jan Eggers, South Dakota's Department Of Tourism, Iowa's Department of Natural Resources, Virgil Beck and *North American Fisherman* Editor Steve Pennaz.

And, a special thanks goes to the NAFC's publication staff for all their efforts: Publisher Mark LaBarbera, *North American Fisherman* Editor Steve Pennaz, Managing Editor of Books Ron Larsen, Associate Editor of Books Colleen Ferguson and Art Director Dean Peters. Thanks also to Vice President of Product Marketing Mike Vail, Marketing Manager Cal Franklin and Marketing Project Coordinator Laura Resnik.

About The Authors

Raised in the small southeastern Wisconsin town of Mukwonago, about an hour's drive from downtown Milwaukee, Joe Bucher began fishing as a young boy in Phantom Lake, near a resort owned by his father. One of two small lakes within Mukwonago, Phantom was noted for largemouth bass; however, it didn't have muskies. Starting with panfish, Joe eventually moved on to bigger gamefish, particularly bass, developing a reputation as a bass fisherman. Meanwhile, Joe would go fishing with his father during vacation trips to northeastern Wisconsin. Their target was walleyes, but the first time Joe caught a muskie, he was hooked on them.

As he grew older, he went into business with his father at the resort. But, a business disagreement resulted in his moving with his wife, Beth, to northeastern Wisconsin where, in 1976, he set up shop as a guide in Boulder Junction. "We starved that first year," Joe recalls. But, now he is one of the top guides in the entire Midwest. The "nose" he developed for locating fish on Phantom Lake makes him an expert guide for walleyes, smallmouth and largemouth bass, northern pike and panfish, as well as his main love—muskies. "Actually, it's relatively easy for a bass fisherman to convert to taking pike and muskies," Joe says, "because he's used to plugging—just upsize a bit in plugs and go for it."

Chicago Tribune Outdoor Editor John Husar calls Joe "the

3

best muskie guide in the business today." His understanding of fish habitat and structure, and his awareness of fish patterns and activity has earned Joe a spot in the book, *Living Legends of American Sport Fishing.*

Joe produces his own radio and television show, "Fishing With Joe Bucher," 26 times a year. In addition to his involvement with the broadcasting media, he works as an editor and freelance writer for the print media. He contributes articles to *North American Fisherman* and two other fishing and outdoor publications, and edits *Musky Hunter Magazine.* Also, Joe has his own line of lures. His wife runs the tackle business which has been built around the Buchertail spinner models, the DepthRaider straight and jointed crankbaits and stranded- and piano-wire leaders and Quick Set Rigs.

Joe also is a frequent speaker at sport-show fishing seminars. And, he hosts fishing schools at Eagle River, Wisconsin, which include three days of intensive classroom and on-the-water instruction for dedicated anglers.

Otis "Toad" Smith (1941 - 1991) became interested in fishing and hunting when he was a youngster, sharing and enjoying the outdoors with his father. Toad got his start in fishing (but not his nickname) from gathering bait for his father's baitshop in Sibley, Iowa. His nickname came from the low-slung crouch he assumed playing on the line in high school football.

A lifelong resident of Sibley, Toad had worked in several occupations, including being a plumber, electrician and deputy sheriff, before becoming an outdoor writer. In 1981, he spent nine

months in Alaska as a security guard on the Alaskan oil pipeline. And, in the fall of 1984, he worked as a guide for elk hunters in Montana.

In January, 1985, Toad suffered a severe heart attack. As a result, he had to have heart surgery which left him physically unable to work. After a year's recovery, he acted upon a good friend's suggestion: to write about his fishing and hunting adventures, and instruct others about outdoor subjects at seminars. Toad immediately began submitting articles to outdoor sports magazines, establishing an outdoor writing career.

Toad wrote articles for *North American Fisherman* and other fishing magazines. In addition, he wrote numerous articles for bowhunting publications. He also held hunting and fishing seminars in Iowa, Michigan, Minnesota, New Jersey and South Dakota. He helped write the book *Catfish Fever* and was the sole author of a book on deer hunting entitled, *Toad's Tricks For Taking Whitetails In the Corn (and Anywhere Else)*.

A popular speaker, Toad held hunting and fishing seminars in the upper Midwest and New Jersey. An unrepentant storyteller, Toad entertained his audiences with many anecdotes including one about using pieces of his own heart (after his surgery) for catfish bait. Toad also was featured in a television piece for "Fishing Iowa." He traveled nationally and internationally, sharing his knowledge and gaining more expertise in the fields of fishing and hunting.

Toad died November 4, 1991, at the age of 50. Despite life-threatening limitations imposed by his heart's reduced capacity, Toad continued to enjoy the days he spent on the water and in the field, including an arduous Montana hunting trip in 1991, and teaching people about the beauty and excitement of the outdoors.

Foreword

Even if I live to be 100, I'll never forget that muggy August night not long ago when Joe Bucher, my younger brother Bob and I fished for muskies on a lake in northeastern Wisconsin. The sun was setting as we launched the boat, but the rising full moon shone with such brightness that the boat cast a shadow onto the calm water.

Joe started the motor and headed the bow due east. "We've been doing pretty well here the past few nights working cranks over weedbeds," he said while handing me a black DepthRaider. "I don't know why, but the action has been starting at 10-till-9 the past few days."

Assuming he was joking, I laughed a bit as I clipped the big jointed crankbait on my line. Most anglers wonder whether or not they will even see a muskie, let alone catch one, and here was a man who was predicting what time he thought the *first* fish was going to hit.

We began working a weed edge near a point, ending each cast with a figure eight. Twenty minutes passed before something slammed my bait just as I ripped it free of a weed. It quickly became apparent that the fish wasn't large, but when I brought it to the boat I was pleased to see it was a muskie, weighing about 8 pounds. Joe reached down with his pliers and removed the hooks without taking the fish out of the water. "Look at your watch," he said while standing up. I was stunned. It was exactly 10-till-9!

The next four hours were unbelievable. We caught and released five more muskies, including a 22½-pounder that gave Bob top honors for the night, before heading back to shore shortly after midnight. A trip of a lifetime for most muskie anglers, but just a good night for Joe Bucher. In fact, two nights earlier he had done the same thing.

Meanwhile, also on a summer trip, co-author Otis "Toad" Smith was having a ball catching trophy-sized pike casting traditional spoons in a northern-Saskatchewan river. The action was hot and heavy until a major cold front moved through the area, pushing the fish out of the shallow bay and shutting down the fishing for everyone except Toad, who switched to slow-trolling dead bait on the bottom of the first deep hole outside the bay. He had caught so many big fish that he had trouble finding any *small* enough to keep.

The point I'm trying to make is that the two authors of this book are not your average pike and muskie fishermen. They are two of the best out there, and their tips will help you catch more and bigger fish. Both of them have written regularly for our official club publication *North American Fisherman*, as well as other well-known, national fishing magazines.

Some of what you are about to read will answer questions you've had for years; some will be contrary to what you have read or heard before. Some of it may even go against what you yourself have experienced on the water. Don't use that as an excuse to discount it, however. These men have put their skills to the test on waters all across North America, and have tried hundreds of different ways to fool fish. Through trial and error, they have culled all but the most consistently successful methods. Those are the ones they share with you today.

This book is for avid pike and muskie fishermen. Thus, you'll notice quickly that the information presented focuses on finding and catching trophy fish. We'll look at the fish themselves, their similarities and their differences. These fish may look a lot alike, but their similarities end there. They spawn at different times, have different water temperature preferences and even prefer different colored baits.

In this book we'll cover pike and muskie fishing in natural lakes, rivers and reservoirs, and cover the water column from top to bottom. Special situations such as dead-baiting early-spring pike will be covered, as well as such things as nightfishing for muskies, something Joe Bucher popularized. And, of course, no muskie book would be complete without a chapter on fishing big suckers for late-fall muskies.

I hope you enjoy *Hunting Trophy Muskies & Northerns* as much as we have enjoyed working on it.

A Special Note: Within days after completing his portion of the manuscript for *Hunting Trophy Muskies & Northerns*, Toad Smith died while on a hunting trip with three pheasants in his hand. I hope I will be so lucky.

> **Steve Pennaz**
> **Executive Director**
> **North American Fishing Club**

Knowing Muskies And Pike

1

The Mystique

T ales of giant pike ripping walleyes off anglers' lines and monster muskies engulfing full-grown loons are but two reasons mystique surrounds these fiery fish. There are dozens, and perhaps, hundreds more reasons. In fact, no other freshwater fish carries the legend and lore that *Esox lucius* (northern pike) and *Esox masquinongy* (muskellunge) do. Much of this is due to their incredibly aggressive nature. They're both efficient predators. It also has something to do with their size. No other freshwater gamefish rivals either of these fish in size potential, though anglers who fish catfish or stripers might argue.

While anglers commonly exaggerate fish size, no matter what species they fish for, lost pike and muskies often carry incredible credentials. Stories of 6- to 7-foot fish are common. In fact, they're a regular occurrence. Even government fisheries personnel occasionally speak of awesome-sized fish being netted or shocked up during surveys. Recently, Wisconsin's Department of Natural Resources (DNR) personnel reported sighting a huge muskie over 5 feet long swimming with a "smaller" fish that was over 50 inches in length. Both fish were temporarily stunned by a DNR boom shocking crew who were evaluating walleye fry survival rates in Middle Eau Claire Lake in the central part of the state. The giant fish recovered from the shock and swam away before the biologist could net and verify its size.

Several other giant pike and muskies have been recorded and photographed by fisheries biologists while working on spring net-

Monster muskies are what the pike-muskie mystique is all about. This awesome fish, caught in the French River, was just shy of 60 pounds. That's a lot of mean fish.

The Mystique

ting operations. One of the most recent sightings occurred during a survey being conducted on Wabigoon Lake in Ontario. Dr. Bernard LeBeau and his team were collecting muskies to be outfitted with radio transmitters to study the habits of larger fish. They did manage to outfit a number of trophy muskies, including several weighing more than 40 pounds.

One day, their long bag (fyke) net captured a huge specimen. After the giant was anesthetized, it was photographed while one technician busily tried to insert the transmitter. Without warning, the monster exploded out of its drug-induced trance and leaped back into the water before the biologist could complete the procedure. Unfortunately, the fish was neither measured nor weighed.

Ah, yes—the mystique lives on.

Recorded world-record catches are mystique-filled in both the size of the fish and the circumstances surrounding the catches. Take, for example, the two largest muskies captured on hook and line; one a 63½-inch, 69-pound, 11-ouncer caught by Louis Spray in 1942 out of Wisconsin's Chippewa Flowage, and the all-tackle world record caught by Art Lawton in 1957 out of the St. Lawrence River, a 64½-inch fish that weighed 69 pounds, 15 ounces. Both of these fish were over 5 feet long, and weighed nearly 70 pounds; both are surrounded by controversy.

As the story goes, Louis Spray, a well-known muskie specialist from Rice Lake, Wisconsin, supposedly spotted the huge muskie he caught on the Chippewa Flowage long before he caught it. In fact, he claimed to have spent weeks trying to bag the monster. Finally, he rigged up a 25-inch sucker on a multi-hook harness and row-trolled it through the big fish's haunt. The monster muskie smashed the big sucker. After a long battle and several gunshots (anglers were allowed to shoot fish back then), the historic muskie was boated. The fish is still the largest muskie ever taken on hook and line from Wisconsin waters and ranks as the second biggest ever caught.

Afterward, rumors began to surface that Spray bought the fish for $50 from a known gangster who, according to some, caught the fish off the shore below the Winter Dam while hiding out from the law. Because Spray had been seen in the company of such characters, the rumors persisted for years. Spray and relatives denied such claims up until his death. No one disputed the size of

Battling a huge muskie or northern pike to boatside is perhaps the ultimate experience in fresh-water sportfishing. It's a challenge that can cause some anglers to panic.

this fish since it was mounted and displayed in Spray's Rice Lake tavern for years before being destroyed in a fire. Skeptics simply questioned whether Spray was the one who actually caught the monstrous fish.

Art Lawton is as well-known in muskie circles as is Spray. He and his wife, Ruth, caught more huge muskies than anyone else, before or since. His biggest catch, however, which was taken in September 1957, is still being questioned by many loyal muskie hounds. Lawton supposedly trolled up the world's largest muskie, along with several other big fish that famous September day, but instead of displaying it for everyone to see, quickly steaked it out and gave it to his brother to eat. When asked why he didn't mount the greatest muskie ever caught, he just replied, "I don't care for mounted fish. I had two of my earlier muskies put up and they're

The Mystique   15 gathering dust in my attic now. Ruth and I don't fish for mounted trophies; we're after the fun and thrills of battling the biggest freshwater gamefish in North America."

Some anglers also wonder why Lawton waited 30 hours before weighing his fish. Some have gone as far as to suggest Lawton wasn't real excited about his catch because he knew of an even larger fish. No one knows for sure, but this controversy still clouds Lawton's incredible accomplishments.

History also records a fish that may have been even bigger than Spray's or Lawton's. Many claim the pot-bellied brute caught years ago by Robert Malo from Middle Eau Claire Lake weighed as much as 74 pounds, but it is not recognized as an all-tackle world record because of a weighing discrepancy. The fish had an amazing girth and still exists in mounted form somewhere in northwestern Wisconsin. The National Fresh Water Fishing Hall of Fame (NFWFHF) board ruled after an extensive investigation to accept it at 68 pounds even, the third largest ever caught. Many still feel, however, that the "Malo Muskie" is truly the largest ever caught on hook and line.

Muskies even larger than these are claimed to have been caught by a variety of anglers before the open season. And, gigantic specimens are regularly reported being sighted by various anglers throughout North America. If the claimed dimensions are even close to correct, some of these muskies are nearly 6 feet long and weigh easily over 75 pounds—perhaps even closer to 100 pounds. These are only stories, yet they add to the mystique.

And, how about huge pike stories? Muskies are often called the largest member of the pike family, but this is not true. It is only in North American record books that the muskie has outclassed the pike. The North American record muskie, as mentioned, is 69 pounds, 15 ounces. The North American northern pike record is a 46-pound, 2-ounce New York fish, taken in 1940. While this is a big pike, Asian and European pike have attained far greater sizes—nearly double! The top six northern pike ever recorded in a list compiled by European fishing experts Jan Eggers and Fred Buller indicates fish ranging from 78 to 96 pounds! A 90-pound, 8-ounce behemoth (68 inches long) ranks as largest ever caught on hook and line. It was taken from Lough Derg in Ireland in 1862 by an angler row-trolling a homemade giant spoon. Many other huge pike have been captured over the years,

Whether you're tangling with a muskie or a pike, your major concern is going to be its teeth. Both species come well equipped, and even some of the toughest lures are permanently scarred.

but not all on hook and line. Interestingly, the International Game Fish Association (IGFA) lists a 55-pound, 1-ounce pike caught in 1986 in Lake of Grefeern, Germany, as its all-tackle record.

In 1930, a 75-pound pike was taken on line in Ilman Lake in what was known as the Soviet Union. Undoubtedly, other huge fish still exist there because few international anglers have really had an opportunity to explore the vast stretches of water throughout the republics that made up the Soviet Union. Now that this massive country has opened its doors somewhat to angling opportunities, it will be interesting to see what transpires. When you consider that many of those waters have never had boats on them, the potential is exciting. Some U.S. anglers have confirmed that great potential exists in that part of the world, reporting catches

European pike are known to be larger than North American pike. This pike was 44 pounds. It took angler Willem Engeleer almost an hour to land it on 7-pound line. Thanks to the catch-and-release method, other anglers can enjoy catching pike this size.

of some trout strains exceeding 100 pounds.

The image of such 75- to 90-pound class pike is hard to comprehend. Though the majority of these super fish were taken before the turn of the century, several pike much larger than the North American record have been recorded since 1960. Most recent European big pike catches have been accurately recorded. Many of these record pike have been tagged and released, and recaptured by various anglers. An elite group of pike specialists now exists throughout Europe. This group is very much like trophy muskie fishermen in North America. The group has the highest regard for its pike just like the muskie fanatics of North America. Hopefully, this same respect will grow for pike in the United States and Canada in the coming years.

The mystique surrounding giant pike and muskies will never

be lost. No matter how big a pike and muskie actually gets, bigger ones always get away. If a few of these 75-pound-class monsters do indeed exist, it's a good bet that they'll win most encounters with anglers since the average tackle used is simply not enough to hold such a fish. A monster of such proportions will do just about anything it wants after being hooked. It will surely take a long time to land, and many obstructions will be in the way throughout the ferocious battle.

However, thoughts of 75-pound class pike and muskies are what fishermen's dreams are made of.

2

Their Similarities And Differences

Telling a muskie from a northern pike is easy. At least, it is to avid muskie hunters and other experienced anglers. Many "weekend" fishermen, however, have trouble telling these two fish apart. What adds to the confusion is that both fish share the same basic shape and, to some extent, the same waters. Plus, some states have introduced the hybrid or "tiger" muskie, which is a muskie/northern pike cross.

Muskies can be distinguished from pike in several ways. Muskies may be barred-spotted or have almost no markings at all. If markings do occur, they will be darker than the background color of the body. Pike, on the other hand, have white or light colored oblong spots against a dark (usually green) background. Another distinguishing characteristic is that only the top half of a muskie's gill is covered with scales, while the gill cover of northern pike is completely covered. Finally, you can count the number of submandibular pores beneath the fish's jaw. Muskie have six to nine on each side; pike usually have five (although three, four or six occur occasionally).

Muskies go through a variety of color phases. The "clear" variety of the muskie is basically just what it sounds like, clear or silver in color. At times, the clear-colored muskie has a faint indication of marking patterns on the posterior one-third of its body. The "spotted" muskie has a coloration pattern in the form of spots. The spots are present on the gill plates the entire length of the body. The spots even seep out onto the tail and other fins.

A muskie crossed with a northern pike produces a tiger muskie. This Iowa angler is holding a tiger muskie that weighed nearly 30 pounds, a state record at the time.

Their Similarities And Differences

The barred version of the muskie has coloration with vertical dark markings on a light background. The barred muskie will also show some spots on the dorsal, caudal and anal fin. Background colors of muskies can vary depending on environment characteristics of the water they inhabit. Geographic location can also play a roll in a muskie's coloration. One marking pattern may dominate in an area, but all three can be present. No matter what the color or pattern of the muskie, the paired fin and caudal fin will have pointed tips. The pike's paired and caudal fins are rounded.

The hybrid tiger muskie has coloration consisting of irregular narrow vertical dark markings on a light background with stripes merging into the back in an interlocking pattern. The sides of a northern pike sometimes exhibit an alternating pattern of stripes and spots, or narrow-paired bars on a light background. But, the tiger's pattern will never resemble that of a pike. The hybrid's paired and caudal fins will also have rounded tips.

In some areas, you'll find "silver" pike which is a mutant color variation of a northern pike. Silver pike, lacking the characteristic spots, have dark to light grayish-blue sides.

Northern pike are found in a wide variety of waters, but the muskie doesn't seem to adapt to as many cold-water environments. Therefore, they have a much more limited range. The northern pike is the only specie of the members of the *Esox* family that has a broad environmental and geographical range. Pike are found on all continents that fringe the North Pole; muskies are confined to a comparatively small area of the North American continent. They range as far north as southern Manitoba, Ontario and Quebec, as far west as North and South Dakota and as far south as Tennessee.

Pike are very adaptable and can live in almost any type of freshwater, including lakes, rivers and ponds. They prefer weedy bays in natural lakes, and weedy, slow-moving rivers. Temperature preferences change as pike grow. Pike under 7 pounds, for example, prefer water in the 65- to 70-degree range; larger pike prefer 50 to 55 degrees.

Both the northern pike and the muskie are ferocious predators, and will feed on just about anything that swims. The pike, however, does seem to be a bit more diversified as to what it feeds on. For example, pike will feed on dead fish, especially in the late winter, and during the cold months of early spring and late fall.

A northern pike (top) bears a close resemblance to its cousins, the hybrid ''tiger'' muskie (middle), and the standard muskie (bottom). If you remember that the pike is light (spots) on dark, and the muskie is dark on light, there should be little confusion.

Their Similarities And Differences

Muskies seldom, if ever, feed on dead bait. Fish are the preferred forage for both pike and muskie, but both fish will feed opportunistically whenever possible. Their diets often include frogs, crayfish, mice, muskrats and ducklings. Both also prefer single, large food items versus several smaller ones.

Both the muskie and pike jaws boast large, sharp, pointed teeth flanked by razor-sharp cutting edges, and the roof of the mouth is covered with short, backward-pointing teeth. This allows them to mortally slash and wound their prey while holding it fast in their powerful, vise-like jaws.

As a predator, the pike is king of its waters. Because the pike has the ability and the looks to be a great predator, it has come to be known by many names. Depending on location, the pike is known as Water Wolf, Toothy Critter, Slew Shark, Snake, or, up in Canada, just plain "Jack."

However, pike and muskies cohabitate very well in regions where the water temperature doesn't get too hot or too cold. In fact, this subject of cohabitation between pike and muskies is open to much debate. Many muskie fishing fanatics have claimed pike and muskies didn't live well together in the same waters. It was also claimed that pike and pike fry ate many muskie fry each spring. This theory was widely accepted because pike spawned earlier, they both used similar spawning habitat, and the larger pike fry would then gorge on the smaller muskie fry.

While this all sounds logical and possible on paper, it's arguable as to whether it actually happens in the real underwater world. Most of the top-rated, world-class muskie waters also contain strong populations of northern pike. Legendary waters such as Lake Of The Woods, Georgian Bay, Lake Wabigoon, Leech Lake, Eagle Lake, Lac Vieux Desert and the St. Lawrence River all have lots of pike and muskies living together in the same waters. The real reason certain waters contain one species and not the other might have more to do with water temperature tolerances than whether the fish was actually native to an individual lake or not.

Artificial stocking of muskies into native pike waters which are within the proper water temperature ranges has been successful in most instances. This casts additional doubt on the age-old theory that pike and muskie cannot cohabitate.

The real reason why muskies don't spawn as successfully

Wood-cluttered shorelines (like this) are good places to look for pike and muskies because they move into the shallows in preparation for spawning in the spring.

numbers-wise in some waters probably has very little to do with northern pike predation. Muskies spawn much later than pike, sometimes as much as a month afterward. In most cases, the bulk of the pike population has moved out of the extreme shallows by this time. Minnow-eating panfish such as crappies and perch might be the real culprits. Egg-eating bottom feeders such as suckers, red horse and a wide variety of chub minnows might also reduce muskie numbers.

Spawning Behavior

Northern pike and muskies both spawn in much the same waters, though pike generally spawn earlier. When ready to spawn, pike and muskies head for the sheltered areas along some shorelines or in the back of bays. They prefer sandy or silted areas over gravel or rocks, and preferably, vegetation should be present. Pike also like to spawn in the dead stems of rushes and reeds at the back of protected bays.

Pike in reservoirs also prefer to spawn in the back of shallow bays among submerged grasses, but they encounter a unique problem. Water levels have an enormous impact on the success of the

Their Similarities And Differences

spawn. If the water drops during the summer months, grasses will sprout on the newly exposed ground. Then, when water levels rise in the spring and cover the grass, it makes for perfect pike spawning habitat. However, if water levels drop after the spawn, pike eggs will be left high and dry. Similarly, if the water levels don't rise again in the spring, most prime pike spawning habitat will be dry and pike will be forced to use less desirable areas.

When the spawning period begins, the males are the first to arrive at the breeding grounds. They may stay there for up to a month; however, the average stay is about 14 days. When the females arrive, their average stay is about 10 days. There is evidence that pike return to the same breeding grounds. In Iowa, where pike and muskies are netted each spring by state crews to be stripped of eggs and milt, tagged fish are caught year after year at the same locations.

Once a female becomes ripe, the shorter male will swim by her side, eye to eye, insuring that the milt he excretes will mix well with the eggs deposited by the female. While mating, the male will repeatedly bump the female by flicking his abdomen against her sides, prompting her to release her eggs. Pike mate every 24 seconds or so, followed by short rest periods. The whole spawning operation can be completed anywhere from one and a half to five or more hours. Two or three males usually attend each female, delivering their mating thrusts from both sides.

Spawning dates can vary from year to year and from location to location. Much depends on the length of the winter and ice-out time. Spawning is stimulated by a rise in water temperature and by increased periods of light. Pike, depending on location, may spawn as early as March or as late as July in areas of Alaska or the Northwest Territories.

Whenever northern pike and muskies do spawn in the same areas at the same general time, natural crossbreeding can occur, resulting in the uniquely marked hybrid tiger muskie, which is a sterile fish. Pike and muskie crossbreeding is most common in shallow, fertile lakes that warm quickly. Spring water temperatures can rocket upward in lakes like this if a streak of hot spring weather combined with strong southerly winds continues for a period of five to 10 days. In this instance, pike probably ventured into a typical warm, marshy cove on the north end of the lake initially, but the wind-driven warm water also set the muskie's

Muskies, as well as pike, love shoreline rocks on a sunny, but cold, day early in the year. The rocks absorb heat from the sunlight, attracting the muskies to shallow, warm water.

spawning urges into high gear earlier than usual. They obviously don't despise each other, or crossbreeding would never occur.

The number of eggs laid by a single pike can vary; it depends upon the size of the female. A small pike may lay anywhere from 25,000 to 50,000 eggs; a pike of 15 or more pounds may lay anywhere from 180,000 to 225,000. The time it takes to hatch the eggs can also vary, depending upon water temperature. Eggs laid in water at 43 degrees will take up to 26 days to hatch. Eggs laid in 50-degree water will hatch in 12 days.

Hatching percentage can range anywhere from 99 percent to nothing. A total loss can occur if the water levels drop. This often happens to the reservoir pike. Cold weather also plays a role in how many pike survive. Severe cold weather can kill the eggs or newly hatched pike. It can also slow the development of other tiny organisms that pike depend on for food during the first weeks of their existence, leaving the fish to starve. Predators also take a heavy toll on pike eggs and newly hatched pike.

Growth Rate

Newly hatched fry don't resemble their parents. They have no fins and their mouths must develop into the familiar duck-like bill. Northern pike fry start out at no more than nine millimeters long. During this time, the fry attach themselves to weeds and grasses, and get their nourishment from an attached yolk sack.

Most pike move to the main lake area during their first 25 days of life. (This is before they have reached an inch in length!) Once out in the main lake they hide in dense vegetation to feed and find cover from predators.

Pike eat heartily and grow amazingly fast. Studies have shown they grow at the rate of .7 inch every 10 days. When they reach 1½ inches in length, scales begin to appear; at 3 inches, their scales are fully developed.

Increased growth coincides with the increased size of the food source. Growth rates vary according to the latitude. In the northern-most part of their range, pike may take seven years to reach 20 inches; 12 years to reach 30. In the extreme southern edge of their range, however, pike can reach 20 inches between the second and third year.

While reaching maturity, pike face many enemies, including some insects like water beetle larvae, and a horde of larger predators. These larger predators would include creek chubs, perch,

Table 1
Annual Growth In Inches Per Year

Location	1	2	3	4	5	6	7
Wisconsin	8	17	23	29	32	36	39
Minnesota	1	13	17	22	26	29	34
Pennsylvania	8	17	24	30	34	38	41
Montana	12	22	29	35	40	42	46
West Okoboji	13	22	29	35	36	38	39
Spirit Lake	9	20	28	32	36	37	39

Table 2
Comparison Of Weight/Length Ratio In Various Areas

Location	30	31	32	33	34	35	36	37	38	39
Penn.	6.6	7.3	8.1	8.9	9.8	10.7	11.7	12.7	13.8	14.9
Mich.	5.8	6.5	7.3	8.1	8.9	9.9	9.9	10.9	12.0	13.1
Wis.	7.6	8.3	9.1	9.9	10.7	11.6	12.5	13.5	14.5	15.5
West Okoboji (Iowa)	6.9	7.6	8.4	9.2	10.1	11.0	11.9	12.9	14.0	14.6
Spirit Lake (Iowa)	6.9	7.5	8.3	9.0	9.8	10.7	11.6	12.5	13.5	14.6

crappies, bluegills, minnows, shiners, walleyes and others.

Northerns live as long as 25 years in the far North, or as long as 16 years in the southern part of their range.

Muskies

Muskies spawn from mid- to late spring when water temperatures range from 49 to 59 degrees. Eggs are scattered at random, usually over some sort of vegetation, and the parents do not stay to guard their offspring as some fish species do.

Muskie fry basically are comparable to pike fry in size and growth rates, and like pike, they have to fend for themselves. Muskie fry also hide in dense vegetation. Not only do they have to protect themselves from the same predators that the pike do, but they also have to stay away from the pike fry.

Studies done by the Iowa Department of Natural Resources show that muskellunge reach 30 inches between their third and fourth year of life. Muskellunge growth in Iowa is comparable to that found inother Eastern and Midwestern states. Growth figures do indicate some variation between states due to latitudinal location. (See Tables 1 and 2.)

Muskies grow more rapidly than the other members of the pike family, and are known to live longer than pike. Females grow faster and live longer than males. (Muskies older than 30 years have been recorded.)

Their Similarities And Differences 29

Finding These
Wily Predators

3

Selecting Prime Waters

N orthern pike and muskie now exist in such a wide range of waters across North America and Europe that listing all the "prime waters" is too difficult. However, there are some noticeable differences between the two, most notably in water temperature tolerances.

In reviewing pike and muskie ranges, it quickly becomes evident that the northern pike's is much larger, yet it does not extend as far south. In the same breath, the muskie is virtually nonexistent above southern Ontario, Manitoba and Quebec, while northern pike are found way up into the Northwest Territories and Alaska. This all means that muskies generally do better in warmer waters, while northern pike flourish in cold waters.

Prime muskie and pike waters also vary greatly according to the angler's wants and needs. One pike or muskie seeker might be looking more for numbers and action, while the other is more serious about bagging a big fish. This is when the term "prime waters" varies the most. Large numbers of each species can be found in many locales. Usually fertile, shallower and warmer waters with a large supply of baitfish such as perch contain big numbers of either pike or muskie. These waters are often characterized by a distinct coffee stain or greenish algae color, and lots of weed growth.

Very high populations of pike or muskie per acre of water are the norm here, but the average size of the fish is relatively small. In these waters, hundreds of aggressive pike in the 20- to 30-inch range might be situated in one weedbed. These waters also might

Fertile, shallow warmer waters produce large numbers of pike and muskies, but the pike especially will tend to be smaller in size. However, working the shallows with a buzzbait can be a highly effective maneuver.

Selecting Prime Waters

hold a dozen muskies that are 30 to 40 inches long.

However, trophy potential is often not as great in these waters. This is not to say that a few trophy-caliber pike or muskie are not present in these waters, but percentage-wise, there's simply not as many. In this case, a trophy hunter might have to catch literally hundreds of pike or muskies before tying into one trophy fish. This might not be a bad way to go about it if "action with a shot at a big one" is what you desire. Yet, there are those elite trophy hunters that would rather concentrate strictly on waters with fewer, but larger, fish. This represents an entirely different situation, both in terms of overall populations of fish, and the time it takes to catch one.

True trophy northern pike lakes are usually clearer and deeper, and often contain trout, cisco and whitefish. They might have a few weedbeds and other shallow cover, but they're only used by the big pike seasonally. In lakes like this one, it's not uncommon for northern pike to suspend deep over large stretches of open water in midsummer. Pike are usually more difficult to catch in these lakes, but the average size is usually much greater—30 to 40 inches. Pike in these deep, clear "trout" lakes usually have proportionately smaller heads, but very thick, girthy bodies, in contrast to bigger pike from shallow, fertile lakes. These pike often have enormous heads, long, thin bodies and big tails.

Deep, clear waters also hold monster muskies. Some of the most immense girths ever recorded on big muskies have come from this type of habitat. Muskies with smaller heads and thick, girthy bodies are the norm here. And, just like their toothy cousin, the northern pike, muskies in these deep, clear waters average larger in size and often suspend over deep, open water areas. They only use shallow cover on a seasonal basis—usually in spring and for a short period of time in the fall.

It's important to review statements made earlier in this chapter about a muskie's habitat range because it applies to its trophy potential. Muskies appear to fare better in warmer waters than pike. This greatly enhances their ability to grow to trophy size in a wider range of water temperatures. For this reason, big muskies are regularly caught in shallow, fertile waters, such as Lac Vieux Desert on the Wisconsin/Michigan border, and Leech Lake in Minnesota. In fact, Lac Vieux Desert has produced the only 50-pound-plus tiger muskies ever recorded, 51 and 50 pounds respec-

You won't find huge muskies like this 51-incher in all waters. Waters should be researched carefully ahead of time to be sure you're fishing in the high-percentage areas.

tively. Yet its pike, though plentiful, are smaller in comparative size. Pymatuning Reservoir in Pennsylvania is another warm, shallow body of water; yet, it has given up countless 30- and 40-pound muskies, and even a 50-pounder. These examples are proof enough that big muskies do very well in warm, shallow waters and, also, in deep waters.

Major river systems, shallow and deep, regularly produce both pike and muskies in trophy sizes. Something unique exists in these special waterways that consistently harbors lunker fish of nearly all species. Neither biologists nor fishermen have a clear-cut answer as to why major river systems continually produce such quality pike and muskies. There are probably many reasons.

The overall volume of water in major river systems supports the age-old claim "big water—big fish." This is much the same as

Selecting Prime Waters

the "gold fish bowl" theory which basically means—the bigger the bowl, the bigger the goldfish will grow. The Mississippi, St. Lawrence, Wisconsin, English, French, Detroit, Niagara, St. Clair, St. Mary's, Winnipeg, Red and McKenzie are all big river systems, covering, in some cases, over 100 miles or more. The sheer size of these rivers alone makes them a prime habitat for big pike and muskies, but other important big-fish benefits are provided by these flowing waters.

A river's current provides an endless selection of vantage points for big predators like the pike and muskie to score easily on a wide selection of prey without expending a lot of energy. They can position themselves in an eddy just outside strong current and ambush baitfish almost anytime. The current continually washes food fish into their lairs. Big pike and muskies have honed their ambushing skills to a fine art in and around current.

Both pike and muskies—even when they're active—seem to like hanging around strong current areas. It's not uncommon to see an angler battling either species below a dam, spillway or falls. They'll rarely hold right in fast water; however, they prefer positioning themselves behind a big rock or downed tree next to the fast water. Active pike and muskie in rivers are commonly caught in these popular hotspots.

Genetically speaking, major rivers appear to contain a strong healthy breed of original strains. A common theory accepted by many professional anglers and fisheries is that all of today's pike and muskies evolved from original strains of native river fish. Such beliefs are easy to validate when you consider what happens whenever flowages and reservoirs are created from these rivers. Giant pike and muskies are regularly caught from such waters. In fact, both the largest muskie and largest pike ever caught in North America came from rivers or their reservoirs: a 69-pound, 11-ounce muskie from the Chippewa Flowage in Wisconsin, a 69-pound, 15-ounce muskie from the St. Lawrence River (on the New York/Canadian border) and a 46-pound, 2-ounce northern pike (U.S. record) from Great Sacandaga Lake, a reservoir on the Sacandaga River in upstate New York. In addition, three of the top four monster pike of Europe (which are far bigger than anything North America has produced)—two 92-pounders, and a 90-pounder—came from the Shannon River in Ireland. This sure casts a strong vote for rivers, doesn't it?

Few anglers pay attention to river muskies. These muskies love to hang behind rocks in strong current. This 23-pounder was feeding on the edge of a fast-water boil when he was taken.

The Great Lakes and their tributaries are worth more than a mention for big pike and muskies, too. All of the Great Lakes have produced some big muskies in the past and certainly still contain a few. Lake Huron's famed Georgian Bay stands alone in catches of muskies weighing over 50 pounds. Annually at least one 50-pound-plus muskie is taken from the Georgian Bay area, which, including its tributaries, includes over 350 miles of shoreline.

Lake Michigan, Lake Superior, Lake Ontario and Lake Huron give up lots of big pike in the 20- and even 30-pound class each year. Certain sections of these waters with conducive habitat are big pike magnets year after year. Northern pike populations appear to be strong and climbing in all of the Great Lakes with the exception of Lake Erie, where pike and muskie populations are surprisingly low. No one really knows why pike and muskies aren't flourishing in Lake Erie, but some experts believe that extensive ditching and diking of its many small river- and stream-tributaries in the mid-1800s destroyed key spawning areas. Interestingly, few anglers are anxious to see propagation of either of these species in this famous walleye factory. Perhaps there's a fear that pike and muskies would put a dent in Lake Erie's thriving walleye populations. However, pike and muskies appear to be coexisting well with walleyes in the other Great Lakes.

Lake Michigan's Bay de Noc sector is noted for its exploding walleye fishery; yet, it's every bit as good for big pike. The St. Louis River tributary of Lake Superior is teeming with walleyes, but pike are present in good numbers, too. Lake Huron's Saginaw Bay is being compared now to Lake Erie as a walleye producer, and pike, in addition to some giant muskies, are literally all over Lake Huron.

Muskie populations in the Great Lakes as a whole are very small. In most areas, these populations are so minuscule in most areas that they probably should be protected by stronger regulations than they are currently, and further helped by artificial stocking. Trophy muskies are sighted on a fairly regular basis, but small and medium-sized fish simply don't exist in sufficient numbers for the species to reproduce successfully.

Perhaps the most unusual big-pike producers of all are the tiny sand pits and quarries throughout Europe. Some of these are less than 100 acres, yet they've produced some of the largest pike on record—several exceeding 55 pounds. The reason for this is speculative, but it's a sound bet that it's because of the deep, cold waters with a good food supply. Public access to such waters was probably limited, which left these few big pike unmolested.

Big muskies in North America have rarely done as well in isolated small waters as pike have done in Europe. Small lakes and ponds can occasionally provide some excellent populations of muskies per acre, but rarely do the fish attain any outstanding sizes overall. A 20-pounder would be considered a real trophy in a lake under 100 acres.

However, there are always exceptions to the rule, and Alois Hanser's 64-pound, former world-record muskie caught in the early 1900's fits this role to a tee. Supposedly, Hanser caught this giant muskie—one of the 15 largest ever caught—out of a tiny 28-acre pothole called Favil Lake in northern Wisconsin. Favil

Small lakes, even though fairly deep, are unlikely spots for trophy muskies. However, they can easily harbor one or two lunker northerns like this 40-plus-incher, particularly in the cooler-water regions.

Lake has never before, or since, produced a muskie of such magnitude. No other officially-recorded muskie over 60 pounds ever came from such a surprisingly small body of water.

Does this mean that other small lakes throughout the northern U.S. and southern Canada could have another muskie like this one? While anything is possible, it's unlikely. If these tiny lakes are deep, they might have more potential to produce one giant northern pike than a big muskie. Many big pike have come from such waters, but lunker muskies have been rare.

Finally, the brackish waters of Europe's Baltic Sea and its many interconnected large lakes and rivers throughout Scandinavia have provided some awesome northern pike, with several exceeding 45 pounds. Strangely, no other mixture of saltwater and freshwater in the world has a reputation for holding any pike at all, yet they seem to grow abundantly in Scandinavia. The Baltic Sea is such a consistent producer of overgrown pike that many worldwide pike authorities consider it No. 1 for record-class fish. There are a few folks from Ireland that would probably argue with this claim, but then again, that's fishing.

Recommended Muskie Waters

Selecting a particular body of water to fish is sometimes a tough decision because so many great fishing waters hold both species. Furthermore, a number of "sleepers"—undiscovered or overlooked hotspots—still exist, even in today's busy, fast-paced world. However, there are some sure bets that are definitely worth your time. Here are several favorites:

The Vilas and Oneida County Lakes in north-central Wisconsin are among the best for both number of muskies, and trophy-caliber fish in the 30- to 40-pound range. A routine artificial stocking program funded largely by scores of local muskie clubs around the state insures annual growth of muskie populations in these area lakes. The actual population of muskies in most of the well-known Vilas and Oneida County lakes is second to none. Some are as high as 10 fish per acre. Nearly a decade of staunch catch-and-release practices developed voluntarily by the majority of visiting muskie anglers has helped provide quality muskie fishing in a number of lakes, including Little Arbor Vitae, Palmer, Tenderfoot, The Eagle Chain, Ballard, Irving, Little Trout, The Minocqua Chain and Squirrel.

In the opposite corner of Wisconsin rests Sawyer County and its legendary muskie waters. Nearly all the state's world-class muskies have come from this area, including the second largest of all time: Louis Spray's 69-pound, 11-ouncer from Chippewa Flowage. "The Big Chip," as it is often called, still ranks as a great piece of muskie water. It continues to produce good numbers, with occasional trophies in the 30- to 40-pound range. An equal commitment to catch-and-release angling has helped keep the Chippewa Flowage alive and well. Nearby Lac Court Oreilles coughed up several record-class fish years ago, including a 67-pounder that is still on display at a tavern in nearby Hayward. Lac Court Oreilles still can be counted on to provide at least one 40-pounder each season. In addition to these famed big-fish waters, a number of smaller lakes that pepper this county contain loads of muskies. A

Complete Angler's Library

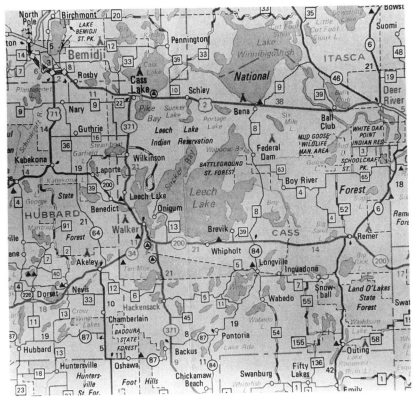

Northern Minnesota's Leech Lake has been known for producing an occasional trophy muskie or pike. Even though its neighbor, Wisconsin, is better known for its muskie and pike fishing, Minnesota has prime waters for both fish.

local favorite of many top area guides is Lost Land and Teal Lakes. Don't overlook Deer and Bone Lakes in neighboring Polk County for hot muskie action, either.

Minnesota's muskie reputation has always been overshadowed by its neighbor, Wisconsin. Still, it definitely has some top-notch waters. Leech Lake, in Northern Minnesota, has given up a number of trophy fish over the years, and it still produces an occasional 30- or 40-pounder. It also has a strong pike population, and occasionally produces trophies. The Little Boy chain north of Brainerd could be the state's best kept muskie secret, but a few professionals might vote in favor of Minnesota's underfished muskie rivers. The mighty Mississippi near Grand Rapids is prime trophy water, while the Big and Little Fork Rivers have stronger overall numbers.

Lake of the Woods, on the Minnesota/Canada border, has to

be one of the top all-around muskie waters in the world, both for numbers and trophies. Its near-one-million surface acres of potential muskie haunts blanket a large portion of southwestern Ontario. Some of the nation's top muskie professionals spend the majority of their time on this particular lake alone. Lake of the Woods has always been a trophy muskie factory. The actual number of 30- to 40-pound fish that come out of this water each season is almost staggering. Yet, it appears to be getting even better. A strong voluntary catch-and-release effort combined with support from the surrounding business community insures that one of our greatest muskie waters will survive well into the next century.

The Canadian province of Ontario is blessed with unequalled trophy-caliber muskie waters. Most of them are located in the southern region. We've already mentioned Lake of the Woods. Other great ones in the western end of the province include Eagle Lake, Wabigoon, Rowan, Dryberry, Pipestone and Lac Suel. However, the eastern side has some of its own legendary waters like Georgian Bay, French, Moon, Miora and St. Lawrence rivers. All of these names have one thing in common—BIG FISH!

The state of Michigan was once considered a prime muskie contender when the late Percy Haver and Homer LaBlanc pioneered speed-trolling plugs and spoons on Lake St. Clair. Awesome photo displays of yesteryear dot the pages of many muskie books bragging up Lake St. Clair's potential. But, Lake St. Clair, which is on the boundary between Detroit, Michigan, and Ontario, went into a muskie-producing tailspin throughout the 1960s and '70s for a number of possible reasons; pollution and over-exploitation are just two of the known culprits. Yet, just when many called Lake St. Clair a "dead sea," it's starting to provide great muskie fishing again. Muskies are coming back strong in numbers, and their size is increasing. And, some smaller inland waters south of St. Clair have gained recent notoriety.

Man-made reservoirs throughout Ohio and Pennsylvania have provided occasional hot streaks of big-muskie activity. Pymatuning Reservoir in Pennsylvania was sizzling hot in the mid-1970s pumping out short, but super healthy, 35- to 45-pound muskies. West Branch Reservoir in Ohio recently was the catch site of an enormous 55-pound 'lunge. Some other notable names worth checking out are Milton Reservoir and Piedmont Reservoir in Ohio, Allegheny and Susquehanna Rivers in Pennsylvania.

Muskies are increasing in numbers, and some of them make it to trophy size, such as this 40-plus-pounder, measuring nearly 54 inches in length. This is partly due to the catch-and-release technique.

Selecting Prime Waters

New York's reputation for muskies is second to none. This is, of course, due to one fish alone, the world record of 69 pounds, 15 ounces, caught by Art Lawton out of the St. Lawrence River. The St. Lawrence's productivity for big muskies is mind-boggling. More 50- and 60-pound-plus fish have come from this single body of water than all others combined. What few anglers realize, however, is that all of these fish were caught when the St. Lawrence Seaway was being constructed. This set up unique circumstances that forced these big muskies out of their normal patterns making them far more catchable. Since the seaway's completion, no more monster fish have been taken.

The St. Lawrence River continues to produce big muskies, but now they're topping out in the 40-pound range. Muskie hunters that have spent years on "The Larry," as it is often called by the locals, claim the fishing is much better now than it has been in two decades. A newly developed stocking program, new trophy protecting regulations (such as a 45-inch minimum size limit), and a catch-and-release attitude by the muskie majority will all help to improve "The Larry" in coming years.

Other spots worth considering in New York state include the Niagara River and the Finger Lakes area. Both produce some quality muskie fishing. Also, the Rudeau River and its flowages have a recently-developed hot, local reputation as muskie producers.

Southern muskie states are starting to gain nationwide notoriety. Dale Hollow Reservoir in Tennessee has a sustaining small muskie population that occasionally pumps out a 40-pounder. West Virginia has a number of small rivers, creeks and mountain lakes that contain fishable muskie populations. Surprisingly, some of the nation's best muskie-lure manufacturers live and test their products on these same West Virginia waters. The state of Kentucky, however, is getting the most play as a southern muskie destination. Cave Run Reservoir is acclaimed by some of the nation's top muskie professionals as water worth fishing. It has a strong population of muskies, and it annually produces trophies in the 30-pound class. Another Kentucky muskie water worth checking out is the Green River Reservoir. Locals claim Green River's muskie population is larger than Cave Run's. Reports of big trophy fish haven't surfaced in the reservoir yet, but the numbers sure seem to be there.

Various stocking efforts have greatly increased the muskie's

With the increased stocking of hybrid (tiger) muskies such as this one, anglers are discovering that these fish exhibit more northern pike traits than traits associated with muskies.

Selecting Prime Waters   45

range. Hybrid muskies are being stocked in limited numbers in over 40 states. States that didn't have a single muskie 15 years ago now have fishable populations. Illinois, Colorado, Iowa, Indiana, Missouri, Kansas and Arkansas all have muskies. Even South Dakota, which didn't have a single muskie 20 years ago, has produced a 40-pound fish. The Canadian provinces of Manitoba and Quebec can also brag of limited muskie fisheries. In some of these areas, anglers had never heard of a muskie until recently. The muskie's range across North America is increasing through artificial introductions. Future catches of outsized lunkers could pop up just about anywhere.

Best North American Pike Waters

The very best northern pike waters contain ample numbers of fish along with excellent trophy opportunities. So, many waters across the U.S. and Canada have great overall numbers of pike per acre of water, but their average size is small. In some cases, these fish are even stunted. These stunted pike are commonly called "snakes" by anglers.

High populations of pike in its southernmost ranges have a larger tendency to stunt than their counterparts in far-northern ranges. This is especially true in shallow, fertile waters. By comparison, deep, cold waters rarely have stunted pike.

Without question, the best northern pike fishing in North America is in Canada. No other country worldwide can compare to Canada's pike fishing opportunities overall. Canada has huge populations of northern pike in so many waters that they're simply too many to name. What's even more impressive is that many of Canada's best pike waters haven't even been fished yet. Fly-in explorations to new wilderness lakes keep revealing more and more underutilized pike opportunities.

Most of the well-known big muskie waters in Ontario, such as Lake of the Woods, Eagle, Nipigon, Georgian Bay, Wabigoon and Dinorwic, produce 40-inch class pike on a fairly regular basis. Smaller, inaccessible fly-in lakes throughout Ontario have even more potential.

The provinces of Saskatchewan, Manitoba, Alberta and Quebec are loaded with premier pike fishing; so much so, in fact, that these waters are too numerous to name. The northern pike is the king of predators throughout these provinces. Muskies are virtu-

In many of the cold, northern lakes, muskies are virtually non-existent. But, the northerns that do grow in those lakes provide great fishing for any angler.

Selecting Prime Waters

ally nonexistent. It's not uncommon to see pike in the 45- to 50-inch category there. Contests held in each of these provinces reveal several 30-pound pike taken annually.

Even the popular trout waters of the Northwest Territories produce some limited trophy-pike fishing. Interestingly, when pike are found in these far northern regions, their size is sometimes incredible. Stories of lake trout fishermen bagging a 50-inch, 35-pound pike are not always fictitious.

The U.S. does have some quality northern pike fishing along with several good trophy opportunities. Some of the hottest big pike action in the past decade or so has come from western reservoirs throughout North and South Dakota. Lake Sakakawea and Oahe Reservoir, and Montana's Fort Dodge Reservoir, have all pumped out huge pike. These highland reservoir pike have lots of deep, open water in which to roam, along with a myriad of quality forages such as gizzard shad, smelt, carp and suckers. More U.S. pike over 25 pounds come from these western reservoirs than perhaps anywhere else.

Northern Minnesota has a number of good pike lakes that have both big populations and some possible trophies. A few of the better known ones are Pelican, Mille Lacs, Leech, Cass and Winnibigosh. The Minnesota side of Lake of the Woods also provides lots of northern pike water, too. The most overlooked big-pike water in Minnesota, however, could be the Mississippi River. Big pike can be caught from its headwaters all the way south to the Iowa border.

The best big-pike waters in Wisconsin is the mighty Mississippi River, especially around the LaCrosse area, but other not so obvious situations abound. A couple of the busily traveled lakes near Wisconsin's biggest cities, Madison and Milwaukee, are surprisingly big-pike producers. Most noteworthy are Lake Geneva, Lake Beulah, Lake Mendota and Lake Okauchee. Flowages of the Wisconsin River in central Wisconsin also have big pike. The best bets are Lake DuBay, Lake Wausau, Castlerock and Petenwell Reservoirs, and Lake Wisconsin. Lots of big pike are also taken around Chequamegon Bay, as well as the St. Louis River (where it enters Lake Superior). The Sturgeon Bay section of Lake Michigan gives up more than its share of trophy pike annually, also.

Michigan's best pike fishing is limited to its bigger waters. Lake St. Clair has tons of pike, but few reach trophy size. How-

ever, several bays and backwaters of Lake Huron are worth fishing. Most notable are areas around Saginaw Bay, Sault Ste. Marie
and St. Martin's Bay, and the Les Cheneaux Islands. A 20-
pounder is possible from any one of these areas.

The best pike waters in the eastern U.S. are without a doubt
connected to Lake Ontario and "The Larry." The Bay of Quinte/
Thousand Islands area is hot pike water. It's doubtful that better
pike water exists anywhere in the United States. Weedbeds along
much of the St. Lawrence River seem almost infested with pike at
times. Still, there are trophies in the river.

The U.S. and Canada have a diversity of good northern pike
waters. Big pike can be taken from the flat desert-like reservoirs of
the western U.S. all the way up and across to the remote woody
wilderness of the Northwest Territories in Canada. If you really
want to catch some big pike, plenty of opportunities abound.

4

Natural Lakes

L ocation of both pike and muskies in natural lakes can vary greatly throughout the seasons. Furthermore, the bigger fish will often be working entirely different areas after spawning than the more numerous small to medium-sized fish. Habitat preferences and food choices can vary greatly between small and large specimens of both species.

When both pike and muskies are present in the same waters in relatively good populations, a wide variety of locational patterns often exists. A school of aggressive smaller pike might control a large portion of a big, weedy bay in the late spring/early summer, but a single patch of weeds growing in deeper water at the mouth of this bay will probably hold one lunker muskie. A cluster of small islands with some weedy saddles and scattered rock might hold pike just about anywhere. However, a muskie working the same island cluster will usually be situated right where the wind and wave action first come into contact with weeds or rocks.

In other words, muskies will usually be on the most opportune ambush point on any given spot. Because of their generally larger size, they will dominate and, consequently, get their pick of choice spots.

Outsized lunker pike carry this same dominance in some cases. This is especially true in waters where no muskies are present. A single big pike, much larger than the rest of the pack, will usually set up a temporary feeding station on the very best position of ambush. The rest of the pack will scatter along secondary choices.

Fall fishing on lakes for both muskies and pike has spawned an almost cult-like following among serious anglers. Fish like this one feed more during the fall than at any other time of the year.

Natural Lakes

Once this pike is caught, another big one will often take its place within a short time. This same "choice spot" principle works with muskies, too.

These few idiosyncrasies such as separation by size, and pecking order dominance are important things to know because they greatly affect an angler's approach to fishing a given lake. The probable locations of each species, and the prospects of where a bigger fish is most likely to be are more easily deciphered after considering these variables. Think about them when reading this chapter. They will continue to "pop up" as important locational influences.

Spring—The Spawn And Early Locations

Several major differences exist between northern pike and muskies during the spawning season. Therefore, each species needs to be dealt with individually.

Northern pike are the first warm-water gamefish to spawn in most natural lakes each spring. Many claim that pike move into the shallows shortly after ice-out, but strong pike spawning movements in creeks, sloughs and river backwaters may even occur before a large natural lake actually experiences complete ice-out.

This phenomenon runs counter to the long-accepted theory that water temperature is the main influence triggering the northern pike spawning migrations because the main lake water temperatures remain unchanged before ice-out. More likely than not, it's an increase in the amount of daylight or some other more subtle seasonal influence that triggers the pike's instinctive urge to propagate.

Even large river and reservoir pike are often sighted spawning in warm-water creeks and small marshy backwaters well before the main river or reservoir has shed its ice. Not all pike spawn this early, but quite a few do. So, a lot depends upon the lake's spawning conditions.

Pike are also very quick and efficient spawners, unlike their close relative—the muskie. They will move into the shallow spawning areas as soon as their reproductive urges begin, and they'll get the job done in a hurry and move out again. This is especially true of lunker females. Big pike will briefly move into the shallows to spawn, and then quickly vacate to deeper waters. Timing a fishing trip to take advantage of this ultra-vulnerable

Complete Angler's Library

Identifying areas where early-spring pike and muskies congregate in the shallows can be a problem in lakes with generally featureless banks. Downed trees are a good tip-off, however.

trophy-pike situation is obviously a tough call. A few days off—either way—and you're sure to miss it.

Spawning areas for pike in natural lakes are often the same as for muskies, and this is why hybridization sometimes occurs when both are present in the same water. Protected areas of warm, shallow water on the north end of a lake are favored. This could simply be a featureless bank in a lake lacking additional topography, but it is more often a small, secluded bay or slough. A number of tiny bays or coves situated at the back end of a large, shallow bay is usually ideal for spawning.

Any cover situated in these warm, shallow waters aids the pike or muskie both for concealment and heat absorption. Concealment and heat absorption are vital to both spawning fish and its eggs and hatching fry. Flats with dead reeds, stumps, fallen trees,

Muskies often will choose the same spawning areas that were used earlier in the season by northern pike. As the water in the shallows continues to warm, you can look for big ones like this to be moving in.

elodea grass, shallow weeds and even bogs are common cover elements in a good, natural-lake pike/muskie spawning area. In fact, many of these same areas will be top-notch crappie, bluegill or largemouth spawning areas after the pike finish.

Ironically, fish biologists have discovered that the Great Lakes muskie (spotted leopard muskie), common only to larger waters, doesn't always spawn in classic warm water bays and sloughs. Instead, the Great Lakes muskies often choose shallow areas with hard bottoms. They've been observed spawning on shallow rocks, sandbars and pencil-grass flats. Occasionally, these spawning areas are even offshore.

In the late 1980s, muskie clubs in Wisconsin, eager to restock Lake Michigan with muskies, found this out the hard way. The Green Bay/Sturgeon Bay area of Lake Michigan had numbers of ideal-looking spawning bays for muskies. A healthy population of northern pike added further confidence to their hunches. Yet, several strong efforts of stocking the native inland Wisconsin muskie in these locations proved futile. But, after being tipped off to this little-known fact about the Great Lakes muskie's spawning tendencies, a new stocking approach was attempted using Great Lakes muskie strains taken from Lake St. Clair in Michigan. Positive results followed.

Historically, very little hybridization has occurred between the Great Lakes muskie and northern pike. These new findings on their spawning site differences provides the answer. They're simply not in the same place during the spawn. It's also understandable why pike and muskies can coexist so well in waters of this nature. They occupy completely separate niches during the spring. In fact, their paths may rarely cross.

Trophy-class pike are extremely catchable during the prespawn/spawn period, while muskies generally are not. Some of the best, early, big-pike catches come on spoons or dead-bait rigs cast to the edges of receding ice. Schools of hungry pike can be found along those edges. Muskies, on the other hand, don't display this kind of activity early in the year. This, again, depicts a distinct difference between the two species. Big-pike purists flock to their favorite waters just before and after ice-out to cash-in on the easy pickings. Few muskie professionals even think of hitting the water until well after the spawn has occurred.

Soon after the spawn, the majority of small to medium-sized pike will set up in nearby cover and immediately relate to some type of baitfish. While many publications have dubbed this time as tough to fish, this simply isn't true. Most pike feed voraciously right after the spawn. If you're not catching pike at this time, you simply haven't found them.

Really big pike are a different subject, however. Nearly all of them are females that go through some degree of stress during the spawn. Afterward, they are noticeably absent for awhile. The duration of this absence depends on weather and a host of other factors. However, a major shallow-water big pike feed usually occurs sometime in the late spring just before these lunkers go deep. Usually, this happens in late May to early June, but it might be as late as early July in the more northern areas. Rampages of big pike in huge schools are often encountered in remote Canadian waters about this time. Anglers who have been in this situation think they have experienced nirvana. Every pike lover in the world should have the opportunity to fish in this situation at least one time in his or her life.

Muskies in natural lakes are more difficult to catch than pike after the spawn, but they can be caught, nonetheless. Small to medium-sized fish are commonly taken on small lures and live-bait rigs by walleye and bass fishermen during this time. These fish hang around reeds, newly emerging weedbeds, downed trees, sunken brush piles and other shallow cover. They feed mainly on perch and other small minnows.

Lunker muskies are almost nonexistent after the spawn. They seem to go through a recuperation period that can last as long as a month or more. Whenever a big muskie is taken during this time, it most often has fallen for a small minnow rather than a traditional big lure.

Summer Pike And Muskie Location

As cold spring nights give way to longer and warmer days, pike and muskie action turns on—big time! An initial streak of early summer heat pushes surface water temperatures upward, concentrating all sorts of baitfish in newly emerging weeds and other shallow cover. Pike and muskie follow inward en masse, and go on one of the best feeding binges of the year.

Natural-lake locations for both pike and muskies are diverse in the early summer. Plenty of fish will be accessible in just about any weed-related spot. Large, weedy bays, weed-coated flats, and weeds on points all have good potential. The best weeds will contain lots of baitfish. However, don't overlook shallow rocks for both pike and muskies, either.

Walleyes ravage schools of minnows and crayfish around shallow wave-pounded rock humps in the early summer. Bigger predators like pike and muskies will be nearby taking advantage of this whole affair, too. They might be feeding on the same minnow/crayfish forage as the walleyes, but the walleyes themselves will be high on the menu of bigger pike and muskies. Large numbers of tooth-scarred walleyes are a dead giveaway here.

Rock humps are productive in many natural lakes across North America, but the humps are most prevalent in Canadian waters. Huge groups of pike can be taken off any given rock hump

By looking at the lake's surface carefully, you can find shallow, mid-lake rock humps. The calm surface in the midst of waves, as shown in the upper lefthand portion of this photo, is what you want to find .

in this situation, but rarely do they measure any larger than 35 inches. On the other hand, muskies over 50 inches will frequent these same rock humps.

Many of a natural lake's biggest pike will totally divert from this shallow warm-water feeding binge and migrate to deep, cold open water forages instead. Trophy pike at this time will commonly inhabit the same locales as lake trout, feeding on ciscoes, tullibees or any other deep-water baitfish. Predictably, it is not uncommon for a lake trout fisherman to stumble onto a monster pike during this period. The biggest pike in the shallower lakes of Manitoba, Saskatchewan and Quebec will simply hold near suspended forage such as whitefish and remain there until the waters cool in the fall.

Activity and location can change dramatically in some natu-

Natural Lakes

ral lakes by mid-summer depending upon the lake's latitude. In far-northern areas that contain pike but not muskies, these fish might continue to be active all summer long, changing their summer locations very little. They could shift slightly deeper in mid-summer, but drastic locational changes probably may not occur. Yet, pike and muskies in southern reaches are subject to longer growing seasons along with much warmer waters. Their locations could change several times throughout the summer period, and the variables here are almost too numerous to mention.

The bulk of pike and muskies in their southernmost ranges suspend over open water at the peak of the summer heat. The biggest pike will separate from the rest of the pack, searching out deeper stretches of open water near cold-water forage. If the water remains fairly clear, free of heavy algae and plankton blooms, pike will continue to feed regularly. However, a thick algae bloom will shut pike activity down a great deal. Short feeding spurts during the brightest portion of midday are most common in this case.

Clear-water muskies will generally be most active during low-light periods and after dark whenever midsummer heat spells prevail. They'll feed regularly over open water during daylight, but many will migrate onto shallow flats after nightfall. Midsummer muskies in darker waters feed intensely, but only for a very brief time just after sunrise and just before sunset. These fish can usually be taken in relatively shallow (less than 18 feet deep) water whenever active.

In late summer (mid- to late August in most regions), the subtle shortening of daylight triggers some strong activity for both pike and muskies. In the northern reaches, these fish might not have ever changed their attitudes noticeably, but southern pike and muskie moods definitely have a very positive turnabout. Many professionals think pike and muskies react to this time period as a prelude to the upcoming fall. Shortening days and cooling nights signal an instinctive response to move inward and begin feeding more often.

Some of the biggest pike and muskies are caught during this overlooked time period. The vast majority of anglers consider these catches flukes, yet consistency demands a closer look. Simply too many "fluke" catches happen during August, year in and year out, to discount its potential.

The approaching full moon of late August seems to have a

strong triggering effect on big pike and muskie movements. In fact, fish activity seems to climax at this time. Dormant deep-water pike of giant proportions are often spotted in shallow weeds. Huge, 50-inch muskies that are not seen for months suddenly follow lures with regularity.

Big tiger muskies also appear to be more active during the full-moon period of late August. More world-class tigers have been caught during this period than at any other time of the year. Strange as it may seem, August continues to be overlooked even though statistics bear out some indisputable facts.

The best locations for August pike and muskies are tied heavily to food sources. Usually, the most productive areas have a multi-forage base. Find a thick bed of emergent weeds on a large, mid-lake flat with visible signs of baitfish activity both in it, and in the deep water nearby, and you're probably going to score big. Patches of deep-water bottom grass on an otherwise coverless clear lake can be a hot number now, too. This deep grass (sometimes growing in waters 18 to 35 feet deep) peaks out in mid-August, drawing in huge quantities of baitfish for the first and only time of the year.

Oddly enough, some of the toughest natural lakes to fish produce the best during the month of August. The biggest pike and muskies in these waters move up onto shallower food shelves and become catchable, which is one of few times during the year. Knowing when this happens and capitalizing on it makes fishing truly exciting.

Fall Locations

Pike and muskies move several times during autumn, because of three distinctly different periods that occur during the fall. These periods are pre-turnover (late August through mid-September), early post-turnover (mid-September through early October), and the late fall/cold-water period (mid-October through ice-up). Each period provides a different set of variables for these big predators. Therefore, each period must be dealt with separately.

A subtle drop in the amount of daylight along with cooler nights signals the arrival of the pre-turnover period. It has a strong effect on all fish including pike and muskies. The stratified layers of different water temperatures that developed within a natural lake throughout the hot summer months start to slowly break down. Lighter, warmer surface waters begin to slowly mix with heavier, cooler waters beneath. A pronounced thermocline—a layer of water 18 to 35 feet deep separating warm, oxygen-rich upper layers from cold, stagnant deep-water layers—still exists, but it's starting to weaken. Eventually, it will dissolve during the constant daily mixing action. And, thus, the annual fall turnover will have begun.

All fish, sensing this seasonal adjustment, begin a migration to the shallows in part to avoid the suddenly unstable depths. Pike and muskies react exactly the same, following the vast majority of open-water fish into the shallows. One of the year's last movements of big fish into the shallows begins, and eventually picks up a full head of steam. Anglers who are alert to this annual occurrence can take advantage of the unequalled big-fish action that exists in shallow water.

The same thick-weeded shallows that began producing in mid-August start to really load up with pike or muskies now. And, as nights become cooler, midday fishing really comes alive. Even inactive pike and muskies remain shallow, clinging tightly to thick weed clumps. Shallow boulders on points and isolated humps become great pike and muskie magnets on warm, sunny afternoons. Fall crayfish migrations center around such spots. Pike and muskies gorge themselves on crayfish, as well as on any other baitfish and smaller gamefish that big, shallow boulder areas harbor at this time. Crayfish, by the way, have rarely been considered a pike and muskie forage, yet the remains of crayfish can be found regularly in the stomachs of both toothy critters.

By mid- to late September, the constant increasing cycle of cooling nights and shortening days takes its toll on the thermocline and it eventually breaks down. Feeding activity is often severely reduced during this part of the actual turnover. It appears that this turnover either stresses the fish, or simply spooks and confuses them. Some anglers and biologists theorize that the sudden upheaval of stagnant bottom silt lowers the lake's pH level dramatically. However, once the lake stabilizes after the turnover, a comfortable pH level returns and feeding resumes. Once this happens, a whole different set of locational options takes shape. The cold, stagnant depths are now enriched with oxygen, and are the same relative temperature as the shallower depths.

When the lake stabilizes after turnover in the fall, pike like this can be found in numerous locations. They follow baitfish schools, and rely upon wind direction and types of plankton.

Baitfish begin bunching up in tightly-grouped schools, often shifting positions daily. Wind direction and the movements of certain types of plankton play a big role in this daily positional shift. Pike and muskies will closely follow these tight little schools of migrating baitfish. Wherever the baitfish end up on any given day, pike and muskies are sure to be nearby. As the mid-fall, post-turnover period progresses, these daily baitfish and gamefish migrations increase.

In one lake, these baitfish may be perch that hug the outside edge of some remaining green standing weeds. On another lake, they might be ciscoes suspended over a deep hole. Both muskies and pike seem to relate heavily to schools of suspended crappies in the fall, too. Fall anglers on Lake of the Woods in Ontario, Kentuck Lake in Wisconsin, and Lake Champlain in New York

Having a good selection of detailed maps is an essential part of finding the pike/muskie hotspots in strange waters. Finding these key spots on a map saves you time and frustration on the water.

have all made such claims about a crappie/pike and muskie connection. Deep movements of bottom fish such as suckers and burbot are yet another baitfish option for big pike and muskie to check out. Huge schools of these fish can often be seen on quality sonar equipment scattering across deep main basins of natural lakes after the turnover. Anglers often misinterpret these sonar readings as being walleyes when they're usually suckers or burbot.

A lot of natural lakes throughout the U.S. and Canada, including the Great Lakes, experience massive fall migrations of emerald shiners—especially by mid-October. Their location is easy to peg by simply watching for flocks of gulls. A typical LCR sonar unit will usually turn black with signals when crossing over one of these shiner concentrations. On a calm morning, it is not uncommon to see the entire lake's surface come alive with these glittering silver minnows. Nearly every minnow-eating predator around is sure to be near a big school of these silvery, soft-finned delights.

Points and bottleneck areas that funnel current from strong wave action become key pike and muskie holding areas by mid-fall. By the time main lake water temperatures move down into the 50- to 59-degree range these two areas are the best overall choices. They provide migrating pike and muskies with excellent ambush opportunities, plus points and bottlenecks disorient baitfish making them more vulnerable. Steep, rocky banks and bluffs near a point or bottleneck can be equally good. Any irregular chunk of rock, single big boulder, downed tree or a small underwater point could be a producer. Pike and muskies can be taken both shallow and deep along such spots. Trolling is probably the best way to catch them.

Once the waters cool below 50 degrees, migrations of both baitfish and predators in natural lakes shorten, and all fish congregate around deep holes. These will be wintering areas for many fish. Both pike and muskies continue to feed aggressively, but migrations shallower than 18 feet are less common. One of the biggest mistakes anglers make at this time is fishing too shallow. Late fall pike and muskies might be catchable in numbers on a few select natural lakes in waters less than 18 feet deep, but far more waters contain them at depths greater than this in the late fall. Deep-trolling crankbaits and live bait are the best ways to take them during this time.

Contrary to popular belief, pike and muskies are not always on the bottom during this late-fall period. If they're still feeding on suspended forage, they might surely be suspended, as well. Keeping a watchful eye on your sonar unit will reveal this possibility. However, bottom-oriented baitfish and gamefish might not always show up on even the best sonar equipment at this time. Make certain you've thoroughly fished a high-potential, deep-water area before discounting it.

The ice-over period emphasizes one of the most significant differences between pike and muskies. At this time, pike are clearly far more active than their striped relative. Pike activity cranks up during the first three weeks of ice-over to an incredible level at times. And, while muskies are occasionally taken through the ice during early winter, they are *not* feeding at anywhere near the in-

Locating Pike After Ice-Out

This illustration shows the different depths within a shallow, weedy bay. Immediately following the ice-out stage, you're sure to find pike here.

tensity level that pike are feeding at.

Strong pike migrations into shallow weeds are common during the first few weeks after a natural lake ices over. The calm, quiet, cold-water setting that once existed as a ceiling of ice covering a shallow weedy bay is evidently attractive to both baitfish and pike. Ice fishermen all across North America eagerly await this time of year, and flock to their favorite "pike bay" as soon as the ice is safe to be on.

Hybrid muskies have proven to be far more active after ice-up than true muskies. Perhaps they have stronger pike tendencies in this respect. Hybrids are so active after ice-up in some cases that special regulations have been developed to protect them on certain lakes. They are often mistaken for northern pike by inexperienced anglers.

Mid-winter pike activity levels and locations can change drastically. Heavy snows, thick ice and decaying vegetation can lower healthy pH levels in many natural lakes by mid-winter. This puts pike and most other fish off-feed. These fish become stressed much the same as they did during the turnover. They simply lay dormant until conditions change.

Large, deep natural lakes with healthy green weeds and a lot of deep-water forage become the best ice-fishing targets during mid-winter. These lakes might never develop this classic mid-winter stress stage. Their crystal-clear waters, thinner ice layers, and minimal snow cover due to their more open, wind-swept topography allows ample photosynthesis to occur all winter long. Weeds and phyto-plankton (plant plankton) continue to thrive throughout the year.

In late winter, reduced snow cover and ice thickness, combined with a lengthening amount of daylight, triggers instinctive movements of pike adjacent to spawning sites. This instinctive migration also activates intense feeding urges. Most areas have closed fishing seasons by this time, usually in March to early April, but the few areas that do offer this late-season, ice-fishing opportunity for pike provide incredible action. Pike literally go on feeding rampages before ice-out. Weedbeds just outside creek mouths or near large flats of dead reeds on a lake's north side are usually "can't miss" spots. If you are fortunate enough to live near such a situation, don't miss out on it.

5

Reservoirs

Pike and muskies thrive in many of the reservoirs across the northern United States and Canada. This is because these bodies of water offer a wide variety of food sources. Smelt, ciscoes, suckers, shad, perch and other varieties of minnows and chubs, not to mention carp, sheepshead and walleyes are all potential prey. Thus, reservoir fish grow fast and large. Reservoirs also offer shallow-water bays for spawning habitat, and cold, deep-water areas for the fish to roam during the summer and fall. Reservoirs are so diversified that pike and muskies can usually find a comfortable water temperature with a food source at any time of the year.

Early-Spring Reservoir Pike

If you expect to be successful at catching reservoir pike and muskies, the first thing you must know is each fish's behavior and how they live in reservoirs. You will have to understand when and where each species spawns, where they go in the heat of summer, and where they end up in the fall. Then, of course, you will have to know what fishing techniques will take pike and muskies at different times of the year.

If you are specifically interested in catching a trophy pike, the pre-spawn, ice-out period is the best time to increase your chances. Muskies, on the other hand, usually do little feeding at this time, even though they also will be moving into shallow water. The pre-spawn period will find big female pike putting on the feed bag as

It doesn't get much better than this! These two anglers display a nice stringer of reservoir pike. In the spring, pike are found in the shallower, warmer waters of the bays.

Reservoirs

they get ready for spawning activity. This is when pike will be at their heaviest weights and in a feeding mood. They will also be in areas that make them more readily available to the angler.

During early spring when the ice on the reservoirs begins to blacken, and melting snow sends fresh water trickling into the reservoir, big female pike and muskies move out of their deep-water haunts and into shallow, warm-water bays to prepare for the spawn. Shallow bays are the first to warm, drawing pike into them first, and muskies arrive a short time later.

You can catch pike with live bait and lures at this time, but dead-bait rigs are better. In fact, they are incredibly effective for catching big pike. Unlike muskies, pike are scavengers. They'll often cruise the backs of bays while there is still ice cover, and pick up any dead fish they find. This will continue well after ice-out. Pike have a very good nose. They can detect a dead fish from a long way away, even in dirty waters.

Some of the largest spring pike are caught just as the ice begins to melt away from shore. The bay may still be covered with ice, but if there is 10 or 20 yards of open water near shore, you will want to be fishing. Unlike some fishing circumstances, the best days to fish in early spring are warm, bright, quiet, bluebird days. These are the days that allow the sun's rays to penetrate and warm the water in the shallow bays. Pike tend to stack up in these comfort zones, and midday is prime time for fishing.

When cakes of ice are still on the bays, pike will often cruise right at the edge of the ice flow. When this happens, try throwing a dead bait onto the ice, then slowly drag it off the flow and let it free-fall to the bottom. A strike will often occur before the bait hits the bottom. If no strike occurs, just put your rod in a rod holder, leave the reel on free spool and wait. As pike cruise, they will sense the dead bait and pick it up.

During the last few years, more American anglers have adopted the European quick-set rigs. Basically, quick-set rigs are two-hook setups on a wire leader. The top hook is adjustable so it can slide up and down the leader to adjust to the size baitfish that is being used. The whole concept behind a quick-set rig is that when a pike picks up the bait you can immediately set the hook. Ninety-nine percent of the time, one or both of the quick-set hooks will be in the pike's mouth, not in its throat (so you can release the fish unharmed).

With today's emphasis on catch-and-release, a quick-set rig can play a large role in successful releases. The old way of fishing dead bait called for a single hook. When a pike would pick up the bait, the angler would feed line to the pike until he or she was sure the pike had the bait in its mouth. Then, the hook would be set. This is an effective way of catching a pike. The only problem is that in most cases the hook would be deep in the pike's throat or even in its stomach. This made it impractical or even impossible to release the fish unharmed.

Another advantage of a quick-set rig is that you will miss fewer strikes. In fact, you will hook most of the fish that hit.

There are two types of hooks used on quick-set rigs. Many utilize treble hooks; but, many use the European-style partridge hooks. The partridge hook is a hook that has a smaller hook welded to its shank. The idea is to sink the small hook into the side of the baitfish, leaving the larger hook exposed. Either a coated or uncoated wire leader may be used with these hooks.

(Be sure to check local regulations before using quick-set rigs. It's illegal in some states to use gang hooks. In those instances, anglers often add a small spinner at the front of the quick-set rig, thereby making it a lure which is legal to use.)

When some anglers look at a quick-set rig, they think that it's a lot of "garbage" to hang on a bait; many wonder if the pike will avoid such a rig. If you're of this school, don't worry. Pike do not know what a hook is; all they see in dead bait is an easy meal. Most good bait shops carry a line of quick-set rigs. They come in various sizes. Some are made with small hooks to accommodate small baits, while others come with larger hooks to accommodate the larger baits. It's up to the angler to match the hook size to the size of the bait and fish that he wants to catch.

If you cannot find quick-set rigs, it's simple to build your own. Many companies offer a wide variety of coated and uncoated leader material. Then, it's just a matter of having some leader sleeves, leader-sleeve pliers and a pair of scissors.

Smelt is one of the favorite dead baits for northern pike. And, the bigger the smelt—the better. Smelt give off an odor that really attracts pike. Many anglers will buy several dozen smelt, sort through them and pick out the biggest ones. If big smelt cannot be found, hook two or even three small smelt onto a rig. Remember, big bait—big fish!

If you cannot find smelt, then dead suckers, creek chubs, ciscoes or mooneye shad will work for pike. Many anglers often freeze any large suckers they have left over from summer fishing trips so they have a supply of bait the next spring. To freshen them, anglers will soak them in scent attractors which help pike locate them faster.

Lively, medium-sized suckers fished in the same manner are as deadly on early-spring muskies as dead smelt are on pike. In fact, South Dakota's first 40-pound muskie came in just this manner. An angler using a lively sucker while shore fishing in April hooked that state's biggest muskie.

Tackle For Spring Pike And Muskie Anglers

Long rods are desirable when fishing live or dead bait because they not only allow long, easy casts, they help insure a better hookset. A long rod helps the shore caster remove slack line when setting the hook, and have better control over the fish.

A couple of other important pieces of equipment for the shore angler are good rod holders and a long-handled landing net. Rod holders will help keep your equipment free of dirt and grime. A holder also keeps the rod up where the angler can easily see it in the event of a strike. It's important to have the reel on free spool so that when a pike or muskie takes the bait, it feels no resistance; otherwise, it will drop it.

Long-handled nets make landing big pike or muskies easier, especially if you are on a high bank or soft shoreline. Many pike and muskies tend to roll over when pulled into shallow water, and a long-handled net will help avoid lost fish.

Where To Fish

Most reservoirs are huge, often running for miles and having hundreds of bays. It can be mind-boggling to some anglers when it comes to choosing one spot to fish. The following tips will help you select the best ones.

Look for a bay that extends a long way back from the reservoir's shoreline. If there is weed growth or some other vegetation such as reeds, pencil grass or tobacco cabbage at the shallow end, all the better. Pike and muskies prefer vegetation for spawning. If you can locate a bay that has a small stream running into it, that's even better. The small stream will be carrying warmer and dirtier

Quick-Set Bait Rigs

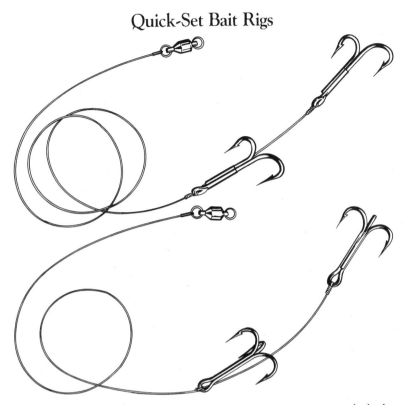

Two types of quick-set rigs are shown in this illustration. With the rig at top, partridge hooks are used while trebles are used in the bottom rig. In each case, seven-strand wire is used to prevent bite-offs.

water. Dirty water collects and holds the sun's heat better than clear water, warming it faster. (It also attracts many spawning minnow species, especially suckers.) Also, look for bays away from the beaten path. Pike and muskies, especially large fish, are very spooky. If there is too much activity and noise in a given area, they will move out.

After ice-out, many anglers like to use their boats to check remote bays. Maps prepared by the U.S. Army Corps of Engineers are excellent for locating secluded bays. Choose bays that offer deep water at the mouth, moderate depths in the middle and a slow tapering shelf running from the back of the bay into shallow water. When checking out a bay, shut off your big outboard motor when you enter its mouth. Switch on the electric trolling motor to quietly make your way to the back of the bay. Find where the bottom breaks from 10 or 15 feet and slopes into the shallows. Then, beach your boat and fish from shore.

After locating a bay that holds the potential of harboring pike or muskies, place baits on the bottom 15 or 20 feet from shore, as well as suspending others below a slip bobber. If there are two or three of you fishing, work as a team. Some lines can be fishing the bottom, while others are suspending. Occasionally, pike and muskies like a bait suspended a couple of feet above the bottom. On quiet, sunny days, you can sometimes see big pike and muskies cruising 3 or 4 feet under the surface as they catch the sun's warm rays. Whenever you see them cruising like that, rig up a slip-bobber rig. It can mean some hot, fast action.

Casting or "wobbling" a dead bait is a uniquely productive method for pike. Hook a dead bait onto a quick-set rig and use only enough weight to sink the bait. Cast the bait as far as you can, let it sink to the bottom and then lift it a few feet before letting it free-fall back to the bottom. Reel in the slack and repeat. At times, this presentation will really trip the trigger of pike. When you feel a pike grab the bait, point the rodtip at the fish, giving it a few feet of line and set the hook when the line tightens.

This "lift-and-fall" presentation also works well when using a slip bobber. Set the bobber so that the bait is suspended 2 or 3 feet above the bottom and cast it as far out into the bay as possible. Then, lift the rodtip up a few feet, while pulling the bobber toward you. Then, feed line to the bobber so the bait settles back down. Continue this lift-and-fall presentation until the bait is in the shallows, then recast as far as possible, again.

Adding Styrofoam to the inside of the dead bait when bottomfishing is another effective presentation. This method is made easy with the use of a dead-bait punch, a tool that is gently inserted in the mouth of a dead bait to make room for a pre-cut piece of 1/4-inch Styrofoam. The Styrofoam is buoyant enough to float the dead bait. Next, hook the floating bait to a quick-set rig and place a sinker a couple of feet in front of the bait. The sinker will take the bait to the bottom. However, the Styrofoam insert will cause the bait to float 2 feet above the bottom. This kind of presentation offers a highly visible bait that is easier for pike to locate.

Besides the dead bait in early spring, various lures will also take pike and, occasionally, muskies. For them to be effective,

Bait Rig For Successful Releases

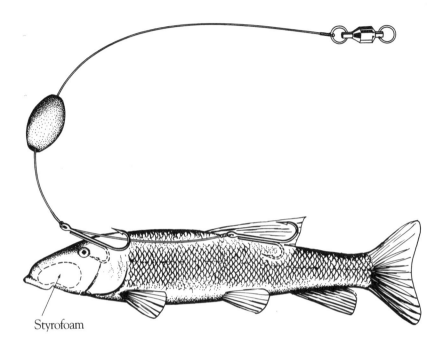

You can add some punch to dead bait on a quick-set rig by inserting a small piece of Styrofoam into the bait, as shown here. The Styrofoam gives the bait a little extra buoyancy that's irresistible to pike.

however, you must work them slowly because neither fish will chase a fast-moving bait. (Remember, their metabolism is geared to the colder water.) Minnow-type baits such as Rapalas or Rebels take early pike in numbers and a once-in-awhile muskie. Select large lures; No. 13 Countdown Rapalas are about right. Go to the back of the bay and cast into the shallows where pike may be holding. Let the lure sink to or near the bottom and slowly retrieve it. Ideally, it should wobble along the bottom kicking up mud. Many times the fish will be attracted to this slow, noisy presentation and scoop the lure right up.

Flash spoons are particularly good early-season pike-getters and underrated for spring muskies. When there is still ice in the bays, throw the spoons onto the ice flows and slowly drag them into the water. Allow the spoons to flutter toward the bottom while you watch your line closely. If the lure stops or the line sweeps off to the side, set the hook. When fishing a falling lure, you often will see a strike before you feel it. If casting a flash spoon, retrieve it slowly and lift and let the lure fall as you retrieve it.

Often, during early spring, cold fronts will move through. When this happens, pike and muskies will pull out of the shallows and hold in deeper water. Shore fishing is futile then. If you expect to catch fish, you will have to change your fishing tactics.

Now is when you will want to make use of your boat and your depthfinder. Move quietly into the bay with the electric trolling motor running and the depthfinder on. You will want to locate the first deep water in the bay. Watch for where the water depth drops down to 20 or 25 feet. In many cases, this is where they will hold—the first deep water near the shallows. You should be able to see the fish holding at the break on your depthfinder.

Once you locate them, it's just a matter of presenting a bait. Put a sinker in front of a quick-set rig and dead bait for pike, a lively sucker for muskies and drop them to the bottom. Troll slowly through the area using your electric trolling motor. This method will produce a lot of strikes. Remember to work slowly. These fish are functioning in slow motion, and a cold front will slow them down even more.

Another presentation that takes pike under cold-front conditions is a heavy leadhead jig baited with a smelt hooked through the head. Drop the smelt-and-jighead combination to the pike and give it a slow lift-and-fall presentation, as if you were fishing through a hole in the ice. Slowly move along the breakline where the pike are holding, using a vertical presentation as you go.

Dead-bait fishing for reservoir pike can last for several weeks after ice-out. Early muskie action with live suckers is always spotty. Reservoirs are slow to warm up. If you start fishing near the end of March, for example, you can usually catch fish until the middle of April. Then, if you travel northern reservoirs, you can experience good shore-fishing into June.

The Summer Period

Once pike and muskies have spawned they go into a period of remission, especially the big females which seem to need a period of recovery. This time period can last for several weeks. Trying to catch a big fish right after the spawn can be next to impossible.

Fishing the shallow bays of a reservoir just at ice-out can be some of your best fishing for pike. This angler caught a beauty using a quick-set, dead-bait rig in shallow water.

You can, however, expect to catch smaller males quite regularly.

Once pike and muskies have spawned, they move back to the deep-water areas of the reservoir, often suspending in a comfortable temperature zone away from shore where they again become catchable. Trouble is, they are scattered. When spawning, they are concentrated in very predictable locations, giving anglers the advantage. Once they take up residence in the deeper waters of the reservoir, it's a whole new ball game. They are no longer concentrated within a small area. Now, it becomes a matter of locating the scattered fish.

An angler also has to realize that reservoirs, such as the huge impoundments of the Dakotas, Kentucky and other states, hold large populations of baitfish. These baitfish may be huge schools of smelt, shad or other fish that usually suspend in the same deep-

Reservoirs

water areas where big predators hold. Pike and muskies can fill their bellies just about anywhere and anytime they want. When an angler is faced with this type of situation, it can make locating big pike and muskies very difficult; catching them is even worse.

Depthfinders Provide Deep-Water Edge

Today's depthfinders give the deep-water anglers an edge that they never had before. Most depthfinders today are very proficient. Not only do they tell an angler how deep the water is, they will show fish. The first step is to locate a school of baitfish; pike or muskies will most likely be nearby. The second step is fishing for them at the depth at which they are holding.

One good presentation for suspended pike is vertically jigging bright, heavy leadhead jigs. It's important to add a stinger hook to catch any fish that strike short or merely swat at the bait. A No. 4 treble hook tied to a 4-inch piece of 20-pound monofilament line that is tied to the jig hook will do the trick. Sharp hooks are also important. Pike have hard mouths, so a sharp hook and a hard hookset are needed to penetrate a large pike's jaw. Large smelt, live suckers or other large live minnows are effective baits.

Another advantage of the depthfinder is that when you locate what you think are pike, you use the depthfinder not only to watch the pike, but also to watch your jig. Once you are over the pike, use your electric trolling motor or slowly backtroll with your outboard. Watch your depthfinder as you drop the baited jig; you should be able to see it go down on the screen of the depthfinder (assuming you have a wide-angle transducer). When the jig approaches the depth of the suspended pike, stop its decent and begin to jig. A sharp 3- or 4-foot lift followed by a free fall is a proven presentation. When you are at the bottom of the fall, let the jig come to a complete rest, then just quiver it a bit and repeat the procedure.

In a lot of cases, you can watch a pike on your depthfinder move toward your jig. When you know the pike is there, it helps you give a more tantalizing presentation. You will have to keep in mind that pike will hit the jig as it free falls or as it reaches the bottom of its free fall. Sometimes, you will only feel a slight "thud" as the pike takes the bait. The vicious strike you were expecting may not occur, so set the hook whenever you feel something "different." Once into the pike, keep resetting the hook without offer-

76

Leadhead Jig With Stinger Hook

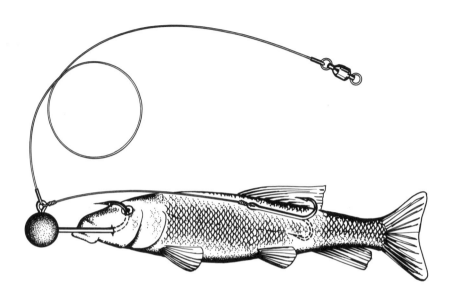

A heavyweight jig with a stinger hook attached, along with dead bait, can be a potent combination for going after pike in deeper water in early summer. Again, a good, heavy wire leader is good insurance.

ing any slack line, maintaining steady pressure.

You will want to use a medium- to heavy-action graphite rod when jigging for pike. A rod must offer plenty of backbone to set the hook into a deep-water pike; yet, it must still have the sensitivity needed to pick up subtle hits. However, not all of the deep-water strikes will be soft and subtle. There are times when pike will hammer a bait. More than one angler while jigging has had a rod torn from his or her grasp by an aggressive pike. It pays to be on your toes at all times.

A real good way to take suspended muskies is to troll deep-diving crankbaits. A combination of lines trolled off planer boards and weighted flatlines is the best approach.

Trolling through deep water can also provide action. Once again, it's a matter of locating the depth where the fish are holding, then trolling your baits at, or just above that level. You can now buy crankbaits that can be trolled down to 35 feet or so, or you can use three-way swivels. Attach an 18-inch dropline to the three-way swivel and tie 2 or 3 ounces of lead to it. Then, tie the lure of your choice to a 7-foot leader and attach it to the three-way. Downriggers are another choice when it comes to trolling deep water. Whatever lure presentation method you choose, use it in conjunction with the depthfinder and practice patience. Realize that big pike and muskies don't come easy.

Besides suspending in deep-water areas in a reservoir, summer pike and muskies will relate to underwater reefs and points. Usually, these underwater humps, reefs and points will attract a certain amount of baitfish and walleyes. Look for this type of structure in the 15- to 28-foot depth ranges.

Once again, a good depthfinder will prove to be invaluable. The depthfinder will point out the underwater structure and, in some cases, show the pike and muskies. Then, it becomes a matter of either trolling a crankbait at the right depth over the underwater structure, or using heavy jigs tipped with minnows to take them. Some days, jerkbaits or bucktails casted over the structure will entice both fish. Most reservoirs have clear water and pike and muskies often will zoom up 10 to 20 feet to take a lure that's above them. Live bait, either slow-trolled or suspended from a slip bobber over structure, can also take plenty of pike. Once again, use big baits. (Big bait equals big fish.)

If you fish summertime pike or muskies in reservoirs, keep in mind that the fishing can be slower than spring or fall, and most of the fish will run smaller than in the spring or fall. But, as a rule, you can still catch enough fish to keep it interesting, especially if you time things right. For example, there is always an intense early-summer feed that takes place with muskies in reservoirs. Usually, these fish bunch up in small groups of three to eight fish, and herd baitfish off points and reefs. This is a great time to take numbers of muskies, along with having a good shot at a trophy. In enticing those muskies, crankbait trolling is your best bet.

The Fall Period

When fall rolls in and the water temperatures of reservoirs begin to drop, the odds of successful pike and muskie fishing tips more favorably in the angler's direction. This is the time when

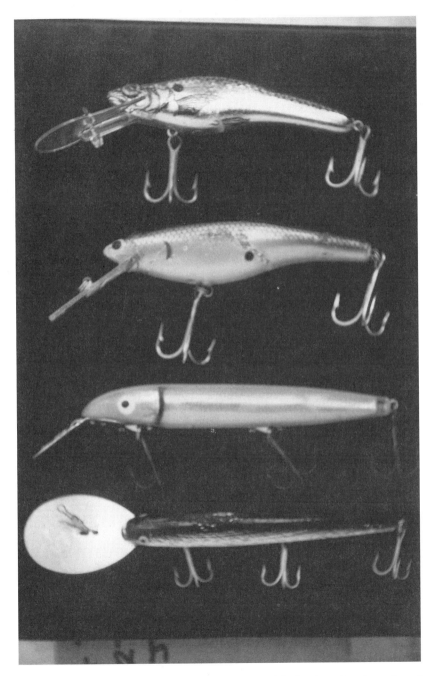

Deep-diving crankbaits like those shown above are some of the best lures for taking pike and muskies in the late summer and early fall. All colors, shapes and sizes seem to be effective.

Reservoirs

these fish move back into the shallow waters of the bays and points and bunch up. Now is when the big fish put on the feed bag.

Fall, especially late fall, can bring some hot action in the bays, off points, shallow underwater ledges, humps or the face of the dam. Because baitfish hang out there during the fall, these places become hotspots. Big predators like pike and muskies will always follow the food source.

When you think of fall pike or muskies, remember that they feed heavily to prepare for the cold, long months of winter. One- and 2-pound walleyes, small pike, large mooneye shad, big 2- to 3-pound suckers or carp are all potential food sources, so are slab crappies. Pike and muskies have big appetites. They will eat anything that they can get into their mouths.

Now serious anglers can concentrate their efforts on capturing a trophy. Make sure your equipment is up to par. A heavy-action, 7-foot, graphite rod with plenty of backbone, lines in the 15- to 40-pound range and wire leaders are "musts." Make sure your leaders are equipped with quality-made, ball-bearing swivels.

Start fishing for fall pike at the mouth of a bay by slowly working your way along the bay's shoreline. Cast your lure right to the bank and retrieve it toward the boat. Continue working the shoreline until you reach the back of the bay, then work your way around the other side. Next, search the center of the bay near the shallow end. Keep casting until you can establish a pattern. If the pike are working the shore, keep casting to the shorelines. If they are holding farther out in the bay, work that area until you have it fished out. Then, move to the next bay and do the same thing.

The face of the dam is also another good drawing card for fall pike and muskies. They will cruise up and down the riprap on the dam's face, picking off baitfish. An angler working a lure off the edge of the riprap can sometimes find hot action. If casting does not produce fish, don't hesitate to try trolling. Troll the dam's face at various depths. Start shallow with a flash spoon for pike, and a big crankbait for muskies.

If no strikes occur, move out to deeper water. Use fairly large lures (6- to 8-inch models are good) and run them in 10 to 12 feet of water. If there are still no strikes, move out into 18 to 20 feet of water and switch to deep-running crankbaits. Change lure color and trolling speed until you find a good combination.

Trolling at various depths as you move into the bays can also

Jigging for muskies and pike with spinning tackle is very productive in the fall, as well as in the spring. This beauty was taken off the edge of a patch of weeds .

Reservoirs

put up big pike and muskies. Hopefully, you will be able to see the fish on your depthfinder screen. Then, it's a matter of choosing a lure that runs at that depth. Change colors and lure speed until you find a combination that works best.

A favorite lure for many anglers in the fall is a leadhead jig baited with a 4-inch grub for pike, or an 8-inch Reaper for muskies. The jig works exceptionally well when casting onto a deep-water point, steep bank or dam face. When casting a point, hold the boat about a long cast from shore. Then, throw the jig up shallow and use a lift-and-fall retrieve as you work it into deeper water. Large, plastic grub bodies are quite buoyant and create a slow, tantalizing fall that pike and muskies find hard to resist. Retrieve the jig until it's directly below the boat, then jig it vertically a few times before you reel it in. This lift-and-fall presentation can be used down the side of a steep bank or down the rock face of the dam. Don't be afraid to try vertical jigging while drifting over rock piles, reefs or along breaklines. Jigs work very well when tipped with live chubs, too.

Soaking a live chub or a big sucker beneath a slip bobber along a point or in the back of the bay will also take plenty of pike and muskies. Try suspending one bait 4 to 5 feet below the surface while you lay the other flat on the bottom. Sometimes, live bait will outfish any artificial lure or bait. When laying the bait on the bottom, use a slip sinker and place a split shot a foot or so above a quick-set rig. Leave the reel in free spool so the pike or muskie feels no resistance when grabbing the chub. Then, as soon as you feel a strike, set the hook.

Live Bait/Dead Bait Combo

The combination of a live bait and a dead bait is sometimes a hot producer, for pike in particular. The dead-bait/live-bait rig works best with the use of a float. Before using this rig, check its legality in the state in which you are fishing because it is illegal in some states. The rig is actually quite simple. It consists of a leader to a hook, then another leader to another hook. On the top hook tail put a live chub; on the bottom hook put a dead smelt.

Suspend the bait combination about 4 to 5 feet below the surface and position the bait on a point a short cast from shore. The action of the live chub will help draw pike to the combination rig. Ninety percent of the strikes will occur on the dead smelt. If pike don't like the smelt, put on a fresh-killed dead chub. This rigging looks cumbersome and awkward, but it will take a lot of pike.

A live chub or sucker hooked through the lips with just enough weight to sink it to the bottom can be worked from a boat in deep-water situations. Slow-troll the live chub over rock piles, humps or reefs. A stinger hook will allow for quicker hooksets. Live bait slowly trolled along the bottom of a bay or in other pike and muskie holding areas is more than they can resist.

Whichever way you choose to fish reservoir pike and muskies, be prepared for some hot action. Reservoir pike and muskies grow big, and they are aggressive. The fishing can be good at any time of the year. It's just a matter of understanding your prey and going after it.

6

Rivers

hile rivers are considered harsh environments, it is fascinating how well pike and muskies thrive in them. Water levels are constantly changing, with high water in the spring and low water during late summer. Water clarity is also constantly changing, which means if a river pike expects to survive, it must be able to catch its prey not only in clear water but in muddy water, as well.

Fishing river pike and muskies is really no different than fishing them in reservoirs or lakes. The only difference is that anglers must cope with currents, water-level fluctuations, changing water clarity and the seasonal movements of pike and muskies. The angler has to know when and where these fish spawn, where they go when finished, where they spend the hot summer months, and where to look for them during the fall and winter.

In this chapter, we are going to deal with fairly large rivers, like the Saskatchewan in Canada and the Mississippi in the states. Even though they are hundreds of miles apart, both rivers, and their fish, have the same habits and characteristics, as do river pike and muskies in other areas of the country. The season dates and food sources may vary from river to river, but the basic fishing techniques are consistent.

Pre-Spawn

When river ice begins to honeycomb and runoff starts trickling in, pike leave their wintertime haunts and begin to stage near

Dead-bait rigs can be dynamite for river pike as evidenced by this nice catch. Most of the lake and reservoir techniques apply to river pike and muskies, but anglers will have to cope with the river variables.

Rivers

spawning areas. Those areas could be the mouths of smaller tributaries or the mouths of shallow sloughs and bays. Pike will enter these areas as soon as the ice melts and water temperatures reach acceptable levels for the spawn to begin. Muskies, which spawn up to a month later, are generally still holding in deep water.

The late-ice period is an exceptionally good time to catch big river pike because they become predictable. Locate these pre-spawn staging areas and the fishing can be fantastic. The fish become more aggressive and feed quite heavily as they prepare themselves for spawning activities. The cold water does slow their metabolism, however. (That's why dead bait is a good late-ice pike bait, especially when it's hanging motionless below a tip-up, or even lying right on the bottom.) Ideally, the bays or sloughs that you fish should have more than one access to the main river. It also helps if there are current and weeds present, especially in the shallow areas.

The River Ice-Out Period

Rivers change dramatically during the spring, much more so than lakes or reservoirs. Melting ice, runoff and spring rains all push river levels up and make the water turbulent and muddy. At this time, rivers can be difficult to fish. Fish are scattered, and the dirty water makes it difficult for the fish to locate the bait. Depending on the weather, it may take a couple of weeks, and possibly longer, for a river to settle down and clear up.

Pike are one of the first fish to get activated by the influx of fresh water and increasing current flow in the spring. As soon as the river begins to break up, they point their noses upstream and begin to move. Some pike will continue to hold in their pre-spawn locations, but others become travelers, heading upstream to find holding areas that provide a break from strong currents.

Muskies, on the other hand, are rarely active to any great degree at this time. Good fishing is still a few muskie weeks away. Prepare yourself for some exciting pike action when the river finally stabilizes and the waters begin to clear. Focus your efforts near natural breaks. Pike will school and hold in these areas as they migrate upstream. Wing dams, points, fallen trees and any other current breaks are good places to try. Sloughs and back bays that have current running through them are also excellent places to try. Two favorite places to catch spring pike are below dams,

Northern pike love to hang around current-break areas in rivers. This one took a jig-and-grub combination that was worked along a small eddy inside some fast current.

and at the mouths of small tributary streams. These two areas will attract and hold more pike than most others.

A good warming trend will push muskies into many of these same areas, where they become catchable for the first time. Huge muskies have been known to surprise walleye anglers that are fishing below the dams at this time.

Fishing Below A Dam

There are a couple of ways to catch pike and muskies below a dam. Some of the Mississippi River dams have areas where the dam butts up against the bank. Usually, a slanted concrete wall separates the dam from the shore. The wall is usually wide enough so that an angler can stand and fish from it, and the wall creates a current break in which pike and muskies like to hold.

Rivers   87

This spot is also good because the dam stops and concentrates migrating fish. The fish will swim along the face of the dam looking for a way through or over the structure. They will eventually move into this area, which makes it a perfect place for an angler to wait for them.

One good method for taking pike (and occasionally muskies) below dams is vertically jigging along the concrete wall. Your lure will need to be fairly heavy so the current doesn't blow it downstream and out of the pike's strike zone. (Remember the pike's metabolism is slow.) Good lures to jig include sonic lures such as the Hedon Sonar, Jigging Rapalas, CastMasters and Swedish Pimples. Sonars seem to work extremely well, offering flash as well as sound waves that pike can hone in on. Use brightly colored lures; they are the most visible in turbulent water. In most cases, it's not necessary to tip the lures with any type of bait. The strikes that you get will be impulse strikes as the lure flashes by the fish at close range.

Other good areas to check are the first current breaks below a dam. When pike get tired of fighting the heavy current at the face of the dam, they will often fall back looking for calm or slack water. Usually, the first calm water pool below a dam will hold resting pike.

Chances are good that you will have to work these current breaks from a boat. Anchor the boat on the edge of the fast water at the head of the hole so that you can cast into the calmer waters.

Several ways are effective in fishing the current break. Dead or live bait on slip bobbers can be floated through the zone. Dead or live bait can be bottomfished in the calm water, or you can vertically jig the break itself. Working a jig tipped with a large grub across the pool can bring fantastic results. Use a jig head that is just heavy enough to get to the bottom, then give it a lift and fall motion as you retrieve it back to the boat. Pay close attention to your line as the jig falls. Chances are you will see the strike before you feel it. When there is any indication of the line jumping or moving sideways in the water, set the hook.

Dams are also good places to fish for muskies during the spring. The easiest way to catch them is by jigging, either vertically or casting with a leadhead jig tipped with a large minnow. Work the entire face of the dam and the concrete sides. Strikes will be subtle, so pay attention.

This large pike was taken by the angler jigging vertically. This is the time to work the faces and sides of dams. Dams are also good places to find muskies, but their strikes will be subtle.

Another great way to take spring pike below dams is with jerkbaits. Surprisingly, a weighted jerkbait worked slowly can be extremely successful on huge muskies, as well. The key is working the area thoroughly before moving on. Working jerkbaits is something shore fishermen can easily do.

The Mouths Of Feeder Streams

Small inlets or bays at the mouths of small feeder streams produce some of the hottest pre-spawn pike activity. Pike will stack up there as they wait for water temperatures to rise before moving up the streams to spawn. The pike holding at the mouth of these inlets or bays are really vulnerable to the angler. Not only are they concentrated, they are usually in a feeding mood. The bay or inlet waters are usually fairly clear, have no turbulence, and water

Rivers

depth runs from a couple of feet down to 10 or 12 feet.

Pike in these bays or inlets can be caught by casting a jig, using the lift-and-fall presentation. They can also be caught on flash spoons as long as you present the spoon with slow, stop-and-fall retrieves. But, if you are serious about catching big pike, you may want to stick to fishing with dead bait. Fishing with dead bait will not be as exciting as casting a lure or jig, but the chances of catching a huge pike are much better. Keep in mind that the pike's metabolism is still slow at this time of year, and easy-to-get meals are very appealing to early-season pike. Pike have very good noses and it's commonly believed that river pike have developed a more effective nose than lake pike. River pike have learned to rely on their ability to sniff out a food source during muddy water conditions. Lake pike can survive by visually locating their prey.

When it comes to fishing for pike with dead bait, enough can't be said about making use of the European quick-set rigs, where legal. Quick-set rigs have already begun to play a large role in modern pike fishing because they are easy to use, extremely effective and help insure the safe release of pike by anglers who practice catch-and-release. A quick-set rig's two-hook setup means that an angler can set the hook as soon as the pike takes the bait. No more waiting for the pike to swallow the hook. The quick hookset will help insure that fish are hooked only in the mouth, making catch-and-release possible without injury to the fish.

Many anglers either hook their dead bait (usually smelt) to a quick-set rig, suspending it from a bobber, or lay the bait directly on the bottom. Then, it's a matter of waiting for a pike to swim by and pick up the bait.

If you want to put a little action in dead-bait fishing you can cast or troll—carefully. Once again, it works best to use a quick-set rig and a long rod. When hooking the smelt onto the quick-set rig, leave it with a slight bow or bend. This way, the smelt will wobble from side to side as it free-falls toward the bottom, or when you retrieve or troll the bait. Sometimes, this slow wobble triggers strikes from otherwise reluctant pike. Adding a scent to a dead bait can also be a plus. Fish Formula II, Berkley Strike, Bait Mate or even WD-40 will help pike find your bait. There is no doubt that on some days the added scent makes a difference.

One of the best ways to fish dead bait is from a boat with a long rod and a quick-set rig. Position the boat in the middle of an inlet

Dead bait is effective when you're trolling for pike. Slow is the key word as far as speed is concerned. Use your electric trolling motor in covering those back bays and inlets.

or bay and cast toward the shore. Then, with a slow, lift-and-fall presentation, bring the bait back toward the boat. In just about every case, the pike will hit the dead bait as it falls or just reaches the bottom of its fall. When a strike is felt, swing your rodtip toward the fish, letting him have the bait for a couple of seconds. After waiting and making sure that you "feel" the fish, set the hook quickly. Fishing this way will help insure you that the pike is hooked in the mouth.

Trolling is another effective way to fish a dead bait in a backbay or inlet. Rig the bait as if you were going to cast it, add just enough weight in front of it to keep the bait down near the bottom and slowly troll the bay, using the electric motor. It's usually best to leave your reel in free spool so that the moment the fish strikes, you can feed some line before tightening up and setting the hook.

Rivers   91

The Spawn

Once the water warms to 39 degrees, pike spawning activity will begin. Muskies, as noted before, spawn a few weeks later. Catching pike and muskies during the spawn is difficult. They have other things on their minds, and eating isn't one of them. As with reservoir and lake fish, catching river pike or muskies during and after the spawn is difficult. The fish won't strike while spawning and it seems as though they need to recover after the spawn. It's not really certain where pike go and what they do after the spawn. Most anglers believe that they back off into deeper waters and recuperate. How much time they need to recuperate is also uncertain. Many fishermen believe that it depends on each individual fish and that the recovery period can be anywhere from two to four or five weeks. For these reasons, NAFC Members are urged not to fish during the spawn. In fact, it's best not to disturb the fish at this time as it may affect the overall success of the spawn.

Post-Spawn And Early Summer

Once river pike and muskies recover from the spawn and begin to feed again, it's time for fishermen to get back on the water. River fishermen have a definite advantage over lake and reservoir fishermen at this time of year. This is because they don't have to worry about the fish heading into extremely deep waters and suspending out in the middle of nowhere. In other words, these fish are easier to find. The range of a river pike isn't much when compared to pike in other bodies of water, especially those in reservoirs. Without having to search as much of an area in rivers, pike anglers are usually more successful at finding them. Some prime searching areas for late-spring and early-summer river pike and muskies are backwater bay areas. The bay or backwater should have enough vegetation at this time, and provide ideal habitat for baitfish and pike alike.

You will find that the backwater areas that hold the most pike and muskies will be ones that have more than one opening to the main river channel. Depending on where the bay or backwater area is located, they can have areas with some fairly strong current. These are the best places to find both species because these waters are cooler and have higher oxygen levels. These types of bays and backwater areas also produce the right kind of vegetation, attracting large numbers of baitfish. In other words, these

Current areas are the best spots for finding both northerns and muskies. This 48½-inch pike was caught in current below the dam in the background on a big muskie crankbait.

areas provide everything that is needed. It's not to say some pike and muskies cannot be caught in bays or backwater areas that have no current, but the ones that do are usually better bets.

When fishing bays or backwater areas that have no current, expect the best fishing to occur right where the bay or backwater enters the river. Fish cruising the river will duck into the mouth of these areas to check them out. Many times, if the water is warm, they only go in for a short distance before heading back out into the river's current.

Muskies also hold in these areas after the spawn. Weedy bays that are adjacent to the main river channel are popular, but big boulders are an even better cover choice. Wood is also excellent cover for spring muskies. Never overlook fallen trees and sunken logs near current breaks. Twitching minnow baits and small jerkbaits is the best way to tempt muskies that are holding in and around wood.

Fishing The Bays And Backwater Areas

Fishing the backwaters and bays during this time of year can be incredible. It's the time of the year that pike and muskies are feeding the most aggressively, and they can be taken by a number of tactics, including casting. It's a simple matter of dropping the electric trolling motor down and working the edge of weedbeds. Chances are they will be laying right in or along the weeds. You will have to choose shallow running lures to stay above the weeds, or lures that dive to moderate depths on the outside edges.

Large spinnerbaits are excellent. They can be retrieved at various depths, and they create vibration and sound waves that pike and muskies can hone in on. Big-bladed baits are preferred because they create lots of flash, making them very easy for pike and muskies to locate. Spinnerbaits are easy to fish. Cast them over the weeds, hold your rodtip high and retrieve them just under the surface. Once past the weeds, pause and let the spinnerbait flutter down 3 or 4 feet, then resume the slow, steady retrieve.

If you are not getting any strikes while casting across the top of the weeds, begin working the edges of the weedline. Cast the spinnerbait near the weeds, let it sink about 4 feet, and retrieve it back to the boat. If no strikes occur, cast the lure back to the outside edge of the weedline and try a lift-and-fall presentation. Let the spinnerbait free-fall a few feet, raise your rodtip and reel, then repeat. The strike can occur at anytime during this presentation.

Jerkbaits like Suicks and Teddys, or large minnow imitators like Rapalas, are also good weedline lures. Jerkbaits can be worked across the top of the weeds or along the edges with good results. Whatever type of bait you choose, remember it will take heavy line and a rod with plenty of backbone to keep a large pike or muskie clear of the weeds. And, don't forget to use a strong leader with a quality swivel.

Wearing a pair of polarized sunglasses can be very beneficial to the angler who is casting weedlines. They will pinpoint your casts, and let you see weedlines and underwater pockets much better.

Another summer muskie technique to try is trolling or casting deep-divers near or over deep boulder fields. A number of huge fish are taken this way every year.

Hot Water And Springs—Great Pike Spots

There comes a period during the hot, dog days of summer when even the water temperatures in backwater areas with good current become too warm for the pike, causing them to look for cooler water. Finding cooler water in a river can sometimes be a difficult task for them. Luckily, they have one thing to fall back on, and that is underwater springs. Underwater springs provide a constant flow of cool water, and the pike will stack up in numbers in these areas.

If you know the location of a few underwater springs in the rivers in your area, give them a try during the summer months. If you don't know where any are, the best way to locate them is during the winter. Many pike can be caught while they are concentrated there. Springs provide cool water during the summer, but they are warmer than surrounding waters during the winter. Often, water just below a spring will not freeze or will have just a thin ice crust, betraying its presence to knowing anglers.

Fishing River Pike And Muskies In The Fall

Fall river pike and muskies are much like fall reservoir and lake pike. When the water temperatures drop, they sense the approach of winter and begin feeding aggressively. They again frequent the backwater and bay areas adjacent to the main river channel. They also stack up below wing dams and other current breaks. Fishing right below dams in the fall can also be good. Fall pike and muskies also tend to roam much more than summer pike. Instead of holding in the weeds, or in the mouth of the bay, they will cruise the weedlines, weedbeds and all areas of the bay as they search for baitfish. Flash spoons such as Dardevles are real good for pike; large crankbaits, jerkbaits and minnow-imitating lures will catch plenty of muskies.

When fishing a bay for fall river pike, start out by working the weedbeds and weedlines with some type of flash spoon. If you're after muskies, start out with a bucktail spinner. Use your electric trolling motor to hold your boat within easy casting distance of the weeds. Cast the spoons over the weeds and down the edges of the weeds. Systematically work the entire weedbed.

Some days you will find these fish holding out in deeper water, often as deep as 15 to 20 feet. Now is when you should switch to large crankbaits and begin trolling. There are enough crankbaits on the market that you can choose a crankbait for nearly any depth range. Manufacturers label the depth that their lures run at. If you are going to be trolling in waters that are 20 feet deep, choose a lure that runs at that depth. You can also control the depth that a lure runs by the amount of line you let out. If the lure is plowing into the river bottom, take in some line. If you think it's not getting deep enough, feed more line.

If you don't have a crankbait that dives deep enough, use a three-way swivel setup with a lure such as a floating Rapala. Attach a 2-ounce sinker with a foot of dropline to the swivel. Then, run a 6-foot leader back to the lure you've chosen. Trolling with this rig is just a matter of dropping the sinker to the bottom and reeling in some line to avoid most snags.

Fall pike tend to congregate in slack water areas adjacent to the main river channel. Muskies, on the other hand, often hold in the stronger current areas, or near them. The depth of these areas will determine how you fish them. If the current is fairly strong, you can vertically jig while drifting these areas with a boat. Hold the jig just above the bottom and give the jig a lift-and-fall motion as you drift. Drifting below a dam while working a jig with a lift-and-fall presentation will also take pike, as well as some bonus walleyes and sauger—and occasionally a muskie. Casting a big jerkbait or minnow-imitation lure within inches of the heavy current or large boulders is a good way to take muskies.

Cold Fronts

Cold fronts can drastically change the behavior of pike and muskies. Plenty of fronts will move through during the fall. These cold fronts usually push the fish back into the first deep water nearest their location. Their feeding pace also slows (muskies even more so than pike). You can catch pike more readily than muskies after a cold front; however, you will have to change your fishing tactics.

On the Saskatchewan River, for example, two anglers were experiencing some fantastic pike fishing. They had located a bay that was teeming with pike, and were having a great time trolling crankbaits and casting. The pike were so aggressive that some of the crankbaits being used were nearly chewed to pieces by the end of the day.

Then, a cold front moved in. The wind picked up; it even

When a cold front passes through, pike usually will hold tight to heavy weed cover, not anxious to chase high-riding lures. This is when a jig is the top producer .

Rivers

A quick-set rig set up with dead bait, such as this smelt, will increase your chances of success when fishing for pike after a cold front.

snowed a bit. Needless to say, the pike-fishing success plummeted with the temperature. In fact, they couldn't buy a strike. Figuring that the pike had pulled out into deeper water, they began to search for them with their depthfinder. They found that they had pulled out to the mouth of the bay and were laying on the bottom.

Knowing that the pike were in a negative mood, these anglers decided to try dead bait. They tied on a quick-set rig, added a 1/4-ounce sinker to the front of the rig and baited up with large, dead smelt. Next, they dropped the electric trolling motor down, and began to slowly troll through the pike. The action was incredible. They couldn't go 10 feet without getting a strike. In fact, they caught more pike slow-trolling dead bait than with crankbaits when the pike were in a more aggressive mood.

The pair caused quite a stir because other boats fishing the same area went fishless. The other fishermen couldn't figure out what this pair was doing. Every time other boats passed them, they were battling big pike. But, they had a problem. They couldn't catch any fish small enough to keep because of the length limit on the river. Now, you may not consider this a problem, but they did. Finally, after releasing a couple dozen pike in the 15- to 23-pound range, they came up with a couple pike that were small enough to take home.

If you're faced with a similar situation involving cold fronts while fishing muskies, search for the holed-up fish and slow troll through the area with large suckers. *Slow* is the key word in getting a response when everyone else has packed up and gone home.

Catching Muskies
And Pike

7

Tackle—Rods, Reels And Line

election of your personal pike and muskie tackle depends
mostly on the type of area you're going to fish, and the size
of fish you will most likely encounter. For example, an
angler who goes on a week-long trip to a remote Canadian lake for pike each summer might only need one or two medium to medium-heavy baitcasting outfits and a box full of spoons
in various colors and sizes. On the other hand, if he also fishes
muskies in northern Wisconsin, trolls the deep, clear waters of
Lake Huron's Georgian Bay, and takes on the big western reservoirs, he might need a pickup truck just to haul his gear around.
The latter angler is the subject of this discussion on selecting the
outfit that's best for you.

Even though all-purpose tackle will work in many situations,
today's avid pike and muskie angler has to become as specialized as
the bass and walleye fishermen if he wants to maximize his success. Different tools to do different jobs is the theme. Pike and
muskie gear is often considered one and the same. Yet, the professionals who fish for both are quick to point out that, while certain muskie tackle catches pike and vice versa, pike tackle differs
very much from muskie gear.

Pike Rods And Reels

The basic function of all the rods and reels discussed here is to
present the chosen bait to your favorite toothy quarry. In other
words, it's simply a matter of picking the right tool for the job at

Long rods are a good choice for pike and muskie fishing. These fish often make sudden, strong efforts to escape at boatside. The extra rod length absorbs this shock, reducing line breakage.

Tackle—Rods, Reels And Line

hand. Because pike lures and live baits are generally smaller than those used for muskies, most of the rod-and-reel combinations and actions are smaller than full-size muskie outfits.

Most pike lures weigh between ½ and 1 ounce. So, big bass outfits should do the job nicely—and they most often do. A medium-heavy action baitcasting outfit or a large spinning combination will handle most pike lures efficiently. (More detailed specifics on actions will be discussed later, but the pike purist should be able to find what he needs to pitch any artificial lure by going through the bass section of a sporting goods store or fishing tackle catalog.)

A perfect rod for spoons and spinnerbaits—two mainstays of the pike angler—is one of the newer, medium-heavy action baitcasting rods in the 6- to 6½-foot range with a long handle. The medium-heavy action works well with most lure weights, while the long handle provides additional leverage for casting, hooksetting and fish-fighting. This same rod works equally well for casting and trolling pike-sized crankbaits. It's just a great all-around pike rod.

The pistol-grip style bass rod, so popular in the 1970s and early '80s, is usually a poor choice, even if the actual rod action is correct. This is simply because it doesn't provide the necessary leverage mentioned before. Hours of casting or trolling big pike lures is sure to tire even the strongest wrist. The added handle length helps distribute the lure's weight during casts and the torque created throughout the retrieve.

Thumb-bar baitcasting reels match best with these rods for pitching pike lures. The thumb-bar is a mechanism that acts as a spool release for casting. Many of today's baitcasting manufacturers offer both thumb-bar and side-button spool releases. The thumb-bar is preferred by many professionals for its one-handed casting capability. Rather than having to reach over and depress a side button for each cast, you can use your casting thumb (already on the spool) to simply engage the thumb-bar lever positioned at the lower end of the spool.

The thumb-bar is also a tremendous fish-fighting aid. A sudden burst at boatside by a big pike or muskie could break a line that had held well up to that point. A reel's drag system rarely is set properly for this kind of explosive interaction, unless the angler purposely resets the drag throughout the battle. A tighter drag setting is needed to set the hook on a long cast and to bull a big fish from weeds. However, a lighter drag is essential on a "green" pike or muskie that strikes at boatside. However, one can quickly hit the thumb-bar into the free spool mode if a pike or muskie explodes at boatside. Then, with light thumb pressure maintained on the revolving spool, line will easily feed out while the speedy pike makes its run.

While a big bass baitcasting outfit is highly recommended for mid- to larger-range pike lures, smaller pike baits are best fished on medium-action spinning gear. But, remember, a short, 5½- to 6-foot spinning rod combined with light line probably means lost fish, especially if you encounter a gator-sized pike. Longer, 6½- to 7½-foot, medium-action spinning rods will turn that advantage around in favor of the angler. The extra length absorbs some of the shock of a pike's lightning-bolt runs, saving both a broken line and a lost fish.

It's also a good idea to look for some special drag features on a spinning reel for much the same reasons covered recently about the advantage of a thumb-bar on baitcasting reels for fighting pike. A drag system that best fits the needs of pike and muskie anglers should include the unique "power lever" feature offered on select models. This "power lever," usually located on the back of a reel right on top of a rear-mounted drag dial, gives the angler the option to quickly reduce drag tension as much as 30 to 50 percent by throwing the lever quickly to the left. Most of the time, this power lever is easily manipulated during the battle with a big fish, and it can prevent broken lines.

Spinning reels containing this power-lever drag feature were popular in the late 1980s, but many newer reels do not have the feature. You may have to search a bit to find such a reel now, but it's worth the effort. If you prefer spinning gear when tackling big pike, the power-lever drag is something to definitely consider.

Spinning reels usually work best for most types of live- and dead-bait fishing for northerns. Most often, friction-free line flow is essential for casting these baits and accompanying hardware. Baitcasting equipment simply will not cast lightweight baits and rigs as effortlessly, or as far, as spinning gear. Some specialized live-bait applications do exist for big baitcasters and northern pike anglers, however, and they will be addressed later.

The very best outfit for live-bait/dead-bait pike fishing is a

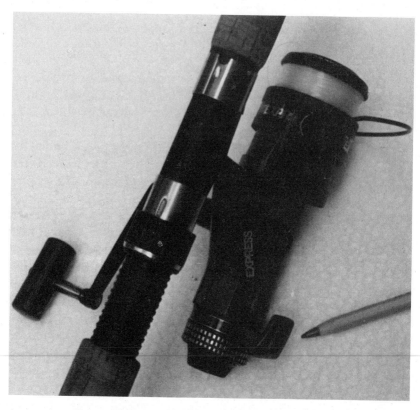

A power-lever drag system (indicated by the pen-point) is a handy feature for the angler who fishes for pike and muskie with spinning gear. Drag can be quickly reduced if a big fish makes a sudden run.

large-spool spinning reel on an extra-long (8½ to 12 feet) European-style rod. The long rod is great for pitching soft-bodied baits long distances without tearing them off the hooks. This is especially important when fishing from shore in the early spring or late fall. The additional length also absorbs shock, helping prevent line breakage when battling big pike.

Few manufacturers make these long rods at the present time. Several mail-order fishing-tackle outlets are doing a great job in this respect, but availability in retail stores is generally poor. Only a few retailers that offer custom rod building supplies have the resources or the knowledge to assist you with this extremely different rod style.

Cold water live-bait/dead-bait pike anglers often fish with a number of rods to maximize their chances. Here's where an audible clicker device on the reel really helps. A number of large baitcasters contain a bait clicker that is often used when fishing large suckers for muskies. This same setup works well when drifting or slow-trolling live or dead baits for pike. In this case, long-distance casting isn't important. One can simply disengage the free spool and gently let out line while the boat drifts or trolls along until the desired depth and line length is reached. The reel is then left in the free-spool position, but the clicker is engaged. This stops any more line flow off the reel until additional tension is applied from either a striking fish or a snag.

A few spinning reels were built with a modified version of the live-bait clicker, but they never sold well, and thus were discontinued. If you can find a spinning reel with one of these gadgets, use it for this style of baitfishing. Most commonly, these spinning-reel bait clickers were referred to as bait sensors, bait runners or bait detectors. They basically served the same function as a clicker on a baitcaster.

Muskie Rods And Reels

The muskie rod business has changed dramatically in the past 10 years or so. Up to that time, the standard muskie outfit was a large saltwater baitcaster matched with a super heavy 5- to 5½-foot fiberglass rod. If you didn't own and use one of these gems, you simply weren't a muskie fisherman. New advances in rod technology combined with trends toward longer rods and lighter weight outfits fell on deaf ears for the most part. Times have changed.

As overall interest in muskie fishing grew in the 1980s, so did a revolution of change in rod and reel preferences. Many of the old-school muskie hunters still stand by their "pool cues," but a trend to longer, lightweight rods and smaller baitcasters has emerged. Powerful, 7- to 7½-foot rods have caught on, in a big way, for a number of reasons.

These new, long muskie rods have very heavy butt sections that taper quickly to a thin tip. They are capable of handling a wide range of lures from ¾ to 3 ounces or so. The heavy butt provides the hooksetting power needed, while the thin tip makes casting lighter lures, such as bucktails, much easier. The thin tip also keeps an all-important bend in the rod during a battle with a big muskie, making it less likely for the fish to throw the hooks.

Tackle—Rods, Reels And Line   107

Long rods, such as this 7-footer, are becoming more popular for muskie fishing. In comparison with short rods, they are easier to use when doing the figure-eight technique at boatside.

This was one of the biggest drawbacks of the old "pool cue" muskie rods. They simply couldn't keep the line taut during the battle, which resulted in lost fish.

The classic boatside technique known as the figure eight is also performed much more easily with a longer rod. Many muskies are caught by alert anglers who draw their lures in a figure eight pattern at boatside upon sighting a muskie following the bait. This figure-eight technique is not easily performed with a short rod, while it's relatively easy with a 7-footer. On the same subject, fewer muskies are lost after striking during a figure eight with the longer rod. The additional length and tip action handles these battles on a short line much more effectively.

Short rods still do have their place in muskie-fishing circles, especially for working heavy jerkbaits in the 3- to 6-ounce range.

The short, stiff action is needed to cast these big baits, and manipulate them properly. Still, there have been improvements made in this style of rod. Today, most are made of high-quality graphite along with newer, lightweight components. The overall weight of these rods is far less than the fiberglass versions with metal reel seats preferred years ago. These newer "sticks" have much greater taper, too, allowing them to bend slightly at the tip during battle. Fewer fish are lost as a result.

Medium-action, 7- to 7½-foot baitcasting rods known generally as flippin' sticks are being used widely by the muskie fishing fraternity now. They work very well for pitching medium-weight muskie lures such as bucktail spinners and shallow-running plugs in the ¾- to 1½-ounce range. These should not be confused with the long rod, which is a medium-heavy to heavy action blank with a very fast taper and stout butt section. These rods, by comparison, have a much lighter action.

Many muskie anglers like the flippin'-stick rod style not only for these small to medium-sized shallow running plugs, but also for jig fishing. Just like the bass angler who often fishes a jig-and-pig with that kind of rod, the muskie man has found the same application with muskie jigs, as well.

These rods pitch all these lures well, set the hook with authority and do a great job fighting a muskie once the fish is hooked. The additional bend in the rod makes it very difficult for a hooked muskie to shake loose, or put any undue pressure on terminal tackle. However, if you're interested in purchasing that style of rod for muskies, make certain you get one with a long handle, preferably at least 11 inches long. Many rods are made with 8- to 10-inch handles, which are simply too short for muskie fishing. The shorter handle length puts stress and strain on the angler's wrist and arms, and severely reduces hooksetting power, leverage and speed.

Lines For Pike And Muskie

A few years ago, line choice for pike and muskies was pretty basic. Muskie fishermen used braided dacron in 30- to 40-pound tests almost exclusively, while pike chasers preferred monofilament in the 10- to 20-pound range. Dacron line had very little stretch, a positive feature for driving large hooks into the tough jaws of bigger fish. Mid-range monofilament handled a wide range of pike

Today, there are many different lines to choose from when fishing for muskies or pike. Shown here are a few of them, including (clockwise from top left) Du Pont's 7/20, Bagley's Silver Thread (17 lb.), Du Pont's 14/40 and Berkley's Braided Dacron.

lures, and worked well on spinning as well as baitcasting reels. That was the extent of line usage and choices.

More recently, line manufacturers have developed very specialized nylons of varying characteristics to fit individual fishing situations. And, while the traditional line choices still do the job, some of the newer products are definitely worth considering under certain conditions. The most difficult thing for the average angler to do now is sort through all the line manufacturers' promotional claims and decipher what he or she really needs. Here are a few suggestions:

Dacron still is a good choice for casting large muskie lures in shallow-water situations, but it is not the best choice when you want a deep-diving lure to reach greater depths. The thick cloth base has a great deal of water resistance and severely reduces the maximum running depth of crankbaits. A far better choice for both pike and muskies is one of the newer copolymer lines. These new lines stretch less than standard monofilament, plus they're 5 to 15 percent thinner. At the same time, copolymer lines are more durable than dacron. One of the biggest drawbacks of dacron has always been its lack of durability. It frays easily; and, once frayed,

Complete Angler's Library

its strength rapidly decreases. Copolymers, while not as tough as traditional monofilament, are tougher than dacron. They have thin diameters and low-stretch characteristics. The best overall size recommendations would be 30- to 50-pound test for casting most muskie crankbaits, and 20- to 30-pound tests for trolling.

Unique copolymer lines that feature flat, oval-like designs for increased casting distance were developed by Du Pont. They are called 14/40 and 7/20. These lines do basically what the manufacturer claims: They spool nicely on a baitcasting reel and cast farther. On the positive side, cpolymer line is an excellent choice for casting, and for many other shallow-water plugs used for pike. The flat-oval copolymer definitely casts these lures well, and they're very abrasive resistant (more so than even standard monofilament). The drawback to this product is that it can't be used on a spinning reel. Spinning reels naturally twist a line as the revolving bail assembly spools the line on the reel. Since this line is flat, twisting it creates all kinds of problems. Also, lures that spin around themselves, such as spoons and straight shaft spinners, cannot be used with this line either. They render this kind of line virtually useless within a few hours of casting. Trolling with these kinds of lures on this line can be a doubly frustrating experience. As long as this line is used exactly for its intended purpose, it will perform beautifully; however, versatility is not one of its traits.

Standard monofilaments still have a place in pike and muskie fishing. Heavy pound tests work great for shallow-water trolling. They provide superior "shock stretch" and durability. Lines in the mid-test ranges are ideal for spinning and lightweight baitcasting. They cast and spool very well on all reels, plus provide that same shock strength and durability essential when using lighter tackle.

8

Tackle—Using Artificial Lures

mong serious big-fish fishermen, it's no secret that pike and muskies are without a doubt the most explosive, tackle-bustin' fish that swim in freshwater. They love to sink their teeth into just about anything that swims by—including artificial lures. Showing no quarter to any style lure, these toothy beasts will chomp down on a metal spoon, a leadhead jig, a plastic crankbait or a wooden topwater plug with equal vengeance.

Therefore, attraction is not a problem. Nearly any artificial-lure style has the potential to take pike and muskies. What one needs to understand, however, is the best lure choice for any given pike or muskie situation depends mostly upon the depth the fish are holding at, and/or the amount of cover they may be holding in. In this respect, all artificial lures are nothing more than tools. The successful pike or muskie angler needs to be able to select the right tool for the job at hand. So, here is an up-close look at these particular tools.

Spinnerbaits And Bucktails

Spinners were made for muskies and pike to destroy! Bass fishermen might argue with this statement, but no bass attacks a spinnerbait with nearly the destructive vengeance of a pike or muskie. Pike and muskies both love spinners in all kinds of shapes, colors, styles and sizes. At times, however, there are distinct differences between productive spinners for muskies versus pike.

Deep-water pike readily attack small jigs rigged with a light-colored plastic tail. Usually, the pike will completely engulf these smaller offerings so a thin-gauge wire leader is required.

Tackle—Using Artificial Lures

Spinners come basically in two styles: the traditional straight shaft and the safety-pin "spinnerbait." You might say that the newly popular weight-forward spinner falls into a third category, but in essence it's still a straight-shaft spinner. Inside these two style classifications is a huge variety of spinners. All the possible combinations of tail dressings, trailers, blade sizes and shapes, and, of course, colors make spinner fishing lots of fun.

The traditional straight-shaft spinner has been a legendary producer for pike and muskie ever since its invention. Small- to medium-sized straight-shaft spinners averaging between 3 and 5 inches long with blade sizes ranging up to about a No. 5 line the tackle boxes of nearly every pike angler around. It's doubtful that anyone heading out on a serious pike trip leaves home without a selection of these killers. Larger versions from 5 to 12 inches long are more popular as muskie lures, and are more commonly referred to as "bucktails." Bucktails have produced more muskies than all other lures combined.

Small, pike-sized spinners are exceptional muskie producers in the early spring before muskies get their big-time appetite. It's not uncommon for someone to bust a real trophy at this time of year while pitching a small spinner for pike or bass. These smaller spinners continue to produce muskies throughout the summer months on lakes with high populations of small to medium-sized fish. In this case, muskies of this size feed on smaller forage overall and are strongly attracted to a small spinner.

Large, straight-shaft bucktail spinners are well noted muskie catchers, but their success on large northern pike is underrated. Whenever pike over 30 inches are available in any numbers, muskie-sized bucktail spinners are better big-pike producers than smaller versions. The 5- to 7-inch versions are particularly effective in bright color patterns.

The biggest difference between straight-shaft and safety-pin styles is in retrieval versatility. The straight-shaft spinner is basically a steady-retrieve lure. Any pause or jerking action stops the blade from spinning. Usually its fish attracting action is greatly reduced whenever the blade quits. The following is a basic rule with straight-shaft spinners: Crank it fast, or crawl it slow, but *always* keep it coming steady.

Safety-pin spinnerbaits were first popularized as bass lures. But, bassers accidentally caught lots of pike on them, and a few

A weight-forward spinner makes an effective trolling lure for both pike and muskies. The front-mounted leadhead eliminates line twist, and the bait dives and spins on turns, triggering strikes.

muskies, too. Soon thereafter, spinnerbaits, with their single upriding hook protected by the overhead wire arm, were one of the most versatile pike and muskie lures ever made for effectively fishing heavy cover. When pike and muskies hang in shallow brush, reeds, bulrushes, lily pads, emergent weeds or any other tough, impenetrable cover, nothing beats a spinnerbait.

Part of the spinnerbait's versatility is evident when a need for changing blades or skirts arises. One basic spinnerbait body can be transformed in skirt color and blade number, size and color in a matter of minutes. Rubber skirts can be changed quickly, and blades can be snapped on and off to suit just about any fishing condition. Additional trailer tails, and stinger hooks can quickly be added, as well. They're simply great all-around lures, especially for pike.

Muskies are most likely to pounce on a bass-sized spinnerbait in the springtime, but larger muskie/big-pike versions have been introduced by several companies. They have proven to be outstanding fish catchers during the warmer months.

Spinnerbaits are also terrific trolling lures. Unlike the straight-shaft version, spinnerbaits will not twist your line. Their shape produces a natural keel keeping the bait upright in the water at all times. On top of that, they are less apt to foul in weeds as they only have one upriding hook. Finally, these lures flutter nicely on trolling turns, which helps trigger following fish into striking.

An almost endless selection of blades is available for today's pike and muskie spinners. To make matters less confusing, stick with larger, rounded blades whenever a shallow-running spinner with quick-lift is desired. Tandem (two blades) spinners simply create double the lift, double the flash, too. Big blades produce a lot more drag making them harder to retrieve. Small and/or long, thin blades usually provide far less lift making them better weapons for slightly deeper cover. Small spinners ride smooth and effortlessly through the water.

A wide array of colors is available on spinners for enticing strikes from both pike and muskies. Generally, the more highly visible colors are best suited for pike, while muskies tend to go for dark hues. A white spinnerbait with hammered nickel blades is tough to beat for pike in clear water. It's also a good muskie producer. River pike and muskies, especially those in stained water flowages, are more responsive to yellow, orange, brown and black skirts (or bucktails) combined with gold, brass or copper blades. Fluorescent blades and skirts are usually best suited for the darker, dingy waters.

Spinners in all their combinations are great shallow-water pike and muskie lures. Matching some of the suggested combinations to conditions at hand should yield consistent results no matter where you fish. Just remember—spinners were made for pike and muskies to destroy! Once you find a productive model, it's a good bet that it won't last long.

Spoons—Pike Simply Love 'Em!

Nearly every angler on earth who has fished for pike knows the "deadliness" of spoons. Something about those funny looking hunks of metal wobbling through the water drives pike wild. Small, medium and large pike from the northern stretches of Canada to the drainage ditches of Holland all love the stamped-metal lures we've all come to nickname "spoons." Spoons come in a wide assortment of shapes, colors and sizes, and probably every spoon made will catch some pike at one time or another. How-

Spoons come in many styles and are designed for nearly every fishing situation. They are espe-cially productive for taking pike. Use magnum models when aggressive, big pike are present; smaller versions work better for small to medium pike.

ever, there's no doubt that some spoons work better than others depending upon conditions. Without getting the least bit techni-cal, here are a few guidelines for NAFC Members to follow when choosing and using spoons for northern pike.

Spoon size depends on the size of the pike available, the over-all number of pike in a given body of water, and the time of year. Generally, big pike like big spoons. The bigger the spoon, the big-ger the trophy. In waters noted for lots of big pike, it's a good idea to stick with very large spoons if you're really serious about bag-ging a trophy. Smaller spoons, in this case, simply attract too many small pike. A big pike can occasionally be caught on a smaller spoon, but it's less likely. Smaller, more aggressive pike, which are far more numerous, will often smash these smaller spoons before a big brute gets a shot at it. A big spoon's profile, however, will discourage smaller pike from striking. They might short strike or follow the huge hunk of metal, but fewer will actually hit it. This gives the hopeful angler a better opportunity to entice a big pike to strike.

Smaller spoons will consistently bag big pike in waters with lower overall populations and heavy fishing pressure. In this case, competition among their own species is not an issue. This is especially common in waters near metropolitan areas that contain fewer, but bigger pike. Here, one big pike might be cruising the open water near a school of suspended baitfish. This fish is both boat-shy and lure-conscious. A small spoon fluttering by on thin, low-visibility monofilament is more attractive now than a giant model attached to a thick wire leader.

In early spring, cold-water pike often prefer smaller spoons, even in remote Canadian lakes. In this scenario, the pike's metabolism might not be geared up yet for much action. The small wobbler size is more attractive now. A magnum-sized spoon might not even draw a follow.

Various spoon shapes, bends and weights produce distinctively different actions and running depths. Wide-bodied, rounder spoons produce a slower, wider wobble, and usually run fairly shallow. This is the most popular style for casting. Heavier versions run deeper, and wobble slower. This concept is the same no matter what style of spoon you choose.

Long, thin profile spoons slither through the water much easier, and display far less lateral wobble. They naturally run deeper and produce a much more subtle action. A heavy, thin-bodied spoon works well when extra depth is needed. It also makes a great vertical jigging lure for ice fishing. A lightweight, thin-bodied spoon works great over the shallows when it appears that pike are short-striking a wide wobbler. An easier target is the answer.

Spoon colors are fun to play around with, and if you study a pike's response closely, you'll often see a noticeable preference for one particular color over another. The classic favorite pike spoon color is red and white, but quite often, it is not the best overall producer. In clear waters, spoons with white and silver are usually No. 1 without fail. Hammered silver with a white pork trailer is "double deadly." But in stained waters, common to many great pike lakes and rivers, yellow or chartreuse combined with a gold brass backside are clearly better. Under the same conditions, a hammered gold spoon with a yellow or chartreuse pork trailer is superb. Another color worth considering is fluorescent red on dark overcast. This pattern will trigger dark-day pike when all other colors draw a blank.

What about muskies and spoons? Well, muskies are certainly caught on spoons. Perhaps more muskies would be caught on spoons if they were fished as seriously as muskie lures. Lake St. Clair guides used spoons as their No. 1 trolling bait for muskies throughout the 1950s and '60s. A resurgence in spoon trolling for Lake St. Clair muskies has taken place more recently. Muskie hunters outside this area simply haven't given spoons the kind of water time that these Michigan trollers have. This could be one of the most overlooked muskie lure techniques of all time. Casting giant spoons over the shallows should take muskies much the same as spinners do. Trolling great big spoons over open water just might be a real sleeper tactic for lunkers.

Plugs, Jerkbaits, Minnow Baits And Crankbaits

Hard-bodied lures of all kinds take pike and muskies in all seasons and at all depths. Each lure category is equally productive. It's simply a matter of selecting the right bait at the right time. Jerkbaits are particularly noted as big muskie catchers, but their effectiveness on big pike is equally as deadly. These big hunks of wood, for some odd reason, trick lunker-class pike and muskies with amazing regularity. They appear to be especially deadly in the fall. No one has ever really come up with a single, good reason why hunks of wood jerked through the water are so irresistible to these toothy fish, but they are.

Buoyant jerkbaits produce a classic up-down action with only a slight lateral movement. They're ideal lures for heavy weed cover. The bump-and-rise movement creates a great strike-triggering action, while at the same time, frees the lure from weed fouling. Usually, buoyant jerkbaits are best fished in warmer water temperatures since they require a fairly fast retrieve. Adding some weight to these lures to decrease buoyancy improves their cold-water capabilities.

Low-buoyancy, torpedo-shaped jerkbaits, often nicknamed "gliders," are versatile lures that can catch pike and muskies spring, summer and fall. They do not work nearly as well over heavy weed cover as buoyant versions; however, their side-to-side

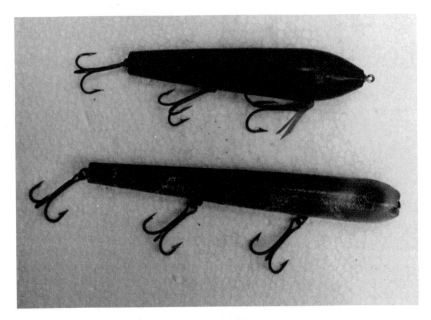

Two examples of jerkbaits for pike and muskies are (top) a torpedo-shaped glider and (bottom) a buoyant jerkbait.

action is simply unbeatable in many other fishing situations. They really shine as pike and muskie producers in the fall. Whenever these fish are hanging around shallow boulders, fallen trees, man-made fish cribs or brush piles, gliders are high-percentage baits. Particularly if a big fish is in the area.

The bigger jerkbaits can weigh as much as a half pound, and therefore require some real stout tackle to be fished correctly. Traditional muskie outfits, such as a pool-cue action 5½- to 6-foot rod with a large-capacity baitcasting reel, and low-stretch line in the 30- to 50-pound range, are standard. Smaller jerkbaits can be fished on longer, more flexible rods.

Long, thin, shallow-running minnow imitations, recently coined "minnow baits," are highly reputed pike and muskie plugs. And, as high as this reputation is, it cannot be exaggerated. These lures are catching big pike and muskies better than ever before. Several guides across the country claim these lures get even more effective following cold fronts or whenever fishing pressure mounts. Their buoyancy combined with a great built-in swimming action makes them excellent, all-around shallow-water weapons for both casting and trolling.

When pike and muskies are deep, crankbaits are one of the best choices for getting them. Crankbaits get down quickly and the pike and muskies love to maul them.

The average angler trying one of these gems on a favorite pike or muskie water will usually cast it out and simply reel it in with a straight retrieve. Nothing is wrong with this approach since it is often all that is needed. However, spooky pike and muskies laying tight to cover after a cold front can be turned onto this bait more so by imparting a short, constant twitching action. Some might compare this to working a jerkbait, but there are subtle differences. A short wrist-twitching action that results in far less forward movement by the bait is desirable. This gives cold-front pike or muskies extra time to look the lure over. The combination of side flash, and short bursts of vibration, along with the diving lip ticking weeds or other cover, is often too much for these high-line predators to resist. Cast a minnow bait near a wavy, wind-blown hotspot, twitch it with a small amount of slack, and you can actually work the lure in-place. This trick will usually fool even the most stubborn fish.

Trolling minnow baits along shorelines, across weedy flats, and off planer boards in open water are all deadly methods. It's one type of lure that's really impossible to fish wrong. It's just that a few tricks make this great bait even better.

When pike and muskies go deep, nothing beats deep-diving crankbaits. They get down quickly to these fish, and pike and muskies both love to tear into them. As a whole, deep divers remain an overlooked secret for both of these gamefish. The bulk of pike and muskie seekers prefer to cast spinners, spoons and shallow-running plugs. Deep-diving crankbaits rarely get the water time that other lures receive.

Crankbait length is important when you're after big fish. Larger, 5- to 9-inch models will take far more lunker-class pike and muskies than smaller walleye and bass versions. This is especially true once the water warms into early summer. Spring pike and muskies are regularly caught on small "cranks," but warming water temperatures stir their appetite for bigger meals.

Jointed models and one-piece versions containing rattles are particularly productive in darker waters and after dark. They emit a lot more noise than straight model divers. In particular, the clicking noises created by a jointed lure's body parts hitting each other has a tremendous fish attracting and triggering effect. It also gives the illusion of speed. This lateral vibration fools pike and muskies into reacting as if the lure is traveling forward faster than it really is. Hard, bone-crushing strikes are very common with jointed lures.

Straight-bodied, one-piece, deep-diving crankbaits are preferred for most clear-water applications during daytime. These baits are especially responsive to faster retrieves and speed trolling. On the other hand, faster retrieves and trolling speeds are not an asset of jointed cranks.

Productive crankbait colors can vary greatly between muskies and pike. Generally, pike are less selective, but appear to react to chartreuse "fire tiger" baits. Natural baitfish patterns that lean toward darker hues are usually more attractive to muskies, but pike will also hit them. Natural perch, natural sucker and black shiner are a few known favorites. Hybrid muskies, which often exhibit many more pike traits than muskie habits, usually go for brighter colors. This is probably why bass anglers tossing brightly colored spinnerbaits catch so many hybrids in the fish's southern range.

The popularity of lipless crankbaits on bass and walleyes should be underscored for pike and muskies, also. These high-speed rattlers turn on bigger predators with the same vengeance. Surprisingly, the pike and muskie angler has overlooked these

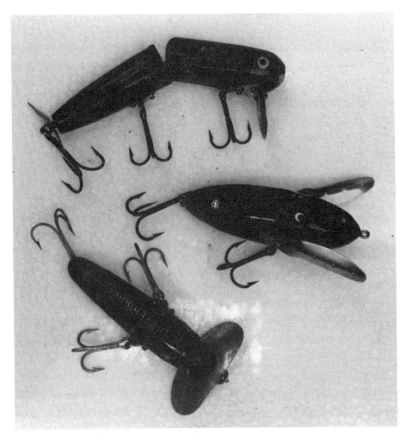

Surface lures entice smashing surface strikes from pike and muskies. The best styles are slow creeper-crawlers like Hawg Wobbler (top), Creeper (middle) and Jitterbug (bottom).

lures. They remain underused. Yet, they're probably the best lure to use for covering shallow water quickly in search of active, feeding fish. If there's a hungry one nearby, it's hard to imagine one not crunching a rattlin', lipless crankbait.

Topwater—Surface Baits

Most bassers brag about their favorite fish's surface feeding ability. And, while it is agreed that bass do indeed hit surface lures with regularity, their classic topwater "slurp" hardly compares to the explosion of a big pike or muskie smashing a surface bait. Plainly put, when a big pike or muskie comes up to take a surface bait, all hell breaks loose.

Just about any topwater bass or muskie lure will take both pike and muskies on the surface, but some work better than others at certain times. Muskies and pike nearly always prefer surface baits worked with a steady retrieve, unlike the productive pause-crank-pause that bass seem to like so well. They'll occasionally crack a topwater bait resting still on the surface, but not as often as a moving one.

Buzzbaits and floating prop-style lures work well in shallow waters less than 8 feet deep. When a lot of water needs to be covered quickly, buzzbaits and prop lures also work best. They are particularly good in warm, summer conditions, and produce well even when there's wave action.

Slower surface baits that produce a great deal of noise with less forward movement are especially productive on trophy-sized fish. They also work better over waters deeper than 8 feet than buzzbaits and prop lures. However, because they require a slow retrieve, fish location is essential. It's best to pitch these lures over known big pike or muskie haunts.

Erratic-action surface baits that produce very little noise are normally poor choices. Even when they do draw pike and muskie strikes, they're missed more than 90 percent of the time. The "walkin' the dog" action is simply too much for pike and muskies. A steady, in-line traveling surface lure is usually a better bet for high percentage hookups.

Jigs: Great Cold Water Lures

Once the water temperature drops below 45 degrees, jigs become weapons worth your consideration. In fact, there are more contest-winning big pike and muskies taken each and every fishing season "by accident" on jigs than any other lure. Popular fish such as crappies and walleyes often school tightly during these times of falling water temperatures, and a lunker pike or muskie is frequently right next to them. It just stands to reason that one will occasionally gulp a small jig retrieved near it.

Recently, a very specialized group of pike and muskie jig fishermen has evolved, and they've fished during cold-water periods with consistent success. Usually, they fish stand-up jigs with big hooks attached directly to light wire leader without a snap. The tails, commonly called "creatures," are usually 6- to 10-inch lizard-like plastic bodies produced both commercially and homemade. Another popular plastic for this style of fishing is the Reaper, which has a wide, beaver-tail profile.

These "creature" fishermen work their jigs off 6½- to 7-foot rods, either spinning or baitcasting. Flippin'-stick rods work great here. A high-visibility line of 12- to 17-pound test is also a must for detecting strikes and visualizing bottom contact on the jig's drop. Instead of lifting the rod and vigorously jigging the lure, experienced jiggers prefer to point the rod low in a hookset position at nearly all times, and simply swim the jig with a few cranks of the reel followed by a pause which allows the jig to drop back toward the bottom.

As simple as this technique sounds, few anglers outside this circle of friends have taken the time to really master it. They basically have this style of fishing all to themselves.

Jigging large minnows, both live and dead, will take pike and muskies during the cold-water periods, too. Large hair jigs, commonly sold for river walleyes, work very well in this respect. So do live rubber bass jigs. They usually have a nice-sized hook, and work well through cover. However, both jigs require a wire leader to prevent bite-offs. Pike and muskies will swallow the entire jig offering nine times out of 10, thereby exposing the line to their razor-sharp teeth.

The most underrated cold-water pike and muskie jigging method right now is the "jig-and-pig"—rigging a live, rubber-legged jig with a big pork-bodied trailer. The jig-and-pig technique that works so well for bass during this time period also takes numbers of pike and muskies. Ardent bassers confirm these hunches with their regular "accidental" catches of big pike and muskies each spring and fall. If more pike and muskie fishermen seriously tried this style of jigging, they would surely catch fish.

9

Shallow Water Techniques

ost anglers instinctively pull a topwater lure out of their tackle box when hot, muggy, calm, low-light conditions exist. Even though this is indeed a good time for topwater baits, other conditions are equally as good. In fact, there are times when they are far more productive than you could imagine.

A classic, favorite topwater scenario is a warm, misty day with no wind. Most professionals prefer this kind of wather as one of the top all-around situations. When calm, misty conditions are proceeded by warm, stable weather, there's even more potential.

Heavy, low-pressure conditions of any kind are high on the list. The very best low-pressure systems for big muskies are usually accompanied by tornado or severe thunderstorm warnings. Obviously, it is not recommended that you go out on the lake and play "Russian Roulette" with bad weather, but lunkers are most susceptible to surface baits during this time.

An overcast day with a light drizzle and a slight chop on the water is also an excellent time, especially when it's backed up by a period of hot, flat days. When the wind is coming from the south and a storm is approaching, it's all the better.

Even though midday can provide some occasional surface bait opportunities, late evening is generally the prime time to fish topwater baits. There is far more surface feeding activity than at any other time during a typical 24-hour period. It's just natural that muskies and pike will be more apt to take a topwater plug

Twitchin' a buoyant minnow bait over thick shallow cover is a deadly way to trigger attacks by both muskies and pike during those tough fishing outings when a cold front exists.

Shallow Water Techniques

during this time than at other times of the day.

A clear, "bluebird" day after a cold front has passed, however, is the toughest topwater condition of all. Once in a blue moon this condition will surprise you. However, most strong northwest winds and bluebird skies usually signal tough fishing on top. If the water you're fishing is gin clear, it will be even more difficult.

Many anglers wait too long before trying surface baits. They think pike and muskies will show interest in this presentation only during the heat of midsummer. Most seasoned topwater anglers, however, are pitching their noisy surface favorites as soon as surface water temperatures climb to around 60 degrees. Once this happens, surface feeding activity really takes off. The initial appearance of baby ducklings is yet another sign. As soon as baby mallards are seen following mama around, surface bait action gets hot. Creeper and Jitterbug-style lures are particularly deadly at this time. They, no doubt, look very much like a baby duckling fleeing for its life.

Slow is the magic topwater word for big-fish success. When it comes to catching numbers of pike and muskies, just about any retrieve speed will catch some, but slow is the best answer for bigger fish. In addition, pike and muskies like steady retrieves. Unlike bass, which often prefer a pause or even a dead, still surface lure, pike and muskies prefer constant movement. Some professionals add a small twitch to the steady retrieve by manipulating the reel handle, hoping to trigger a big follower into striking. It's also important to pay more attention to where casts are placed. Try to spread casts out more when a big fish is present. Never cast your lure near another angler's lure. It will either confuse or turn off a big pike or muskie.

Different surface lures require variances in retrieve speeds to be at their optimum effectiveness. High-action wobblers are best cranked very slowly over glassy, calm water. A slight ripple is still okay, but heavy waves generally are not. A prop-style or buzzbait works well in calm water, but can be even more effective in waves. In fact, jumping over waves accentuates their action.

Changing directions with a topwater lure produces a lot more strikes from a close follower. Long rods help to create distinct turns and angles throughout the retrieve. Thus, most topwater professionals prefer medium-heavy action, 6½- to 7½-foot rods. These longer rods also do a better job of lifting line off the water

Buzzbaits are great topwater lures for both pike and muskies. These baits work well in both calm and choppy waters. Remember to set the hook only after you feel the fish on the line.

when working a prop bait. This increases the amount of noise. It's also important to remember that extra-heavy wire leaders ruin the action of many topwater lures. It forces the nose of the bait downward. This really kills the effectiveness of a front-mounted prop on some lures. Stick with a light-gauge wire and a small ball-bearing swivel.

Perhaps the most controversial part of topwater angling for pike and muskies is timing the hookset. Novices usually set the hook as soon as they see or hear a splash. This normally results in missed strikes. Setting the hook only after feeling the fish pulling on the line or actually seeing it take the bait is a much better policy. Keep your eyes on the action at all times. Occasionally, you won't actually feel the fish with the bait even though it has taken it solidly. In this case, watch for the lure to disappear. If it's gone, set the hook.

Try "Trigger Baits" When They Get Lockjaw

When pike and muskies follow but won't strike, usually a stronger "triggering" method is in order. These fish simply need something more than a basic spoon or bucktail spinner cranked through the water with a straight retrieve. Here, twitchin' floating minnow baits is usually the answer. This is not to say that spoons and spinners aren't good baits. These lures have taken thousands of big pike and muskies. However, experience suggests that once pike and muskies have been exposed to spoons and spinners for a few years, these lures tend to lose some of their effectiveness. Here's where something with an erratic, stop-and-go action will trigger more strikes.

Twitchin' is one of the most unique big pike and muskie triggering tactics developed lately. Twitchin' was coined by northern Wisconsin muskie guides and is appropriately named because the lure, a 5- to 7-inch, minnow-shaped, shallow-running plug, is manipulated with a twitch-like wrist action. This makes the minnow bait dart, dive and flash through all kinds of cover. Twitchin' is especially effective when fish are holding tight to shallow cover after cold fronts. Those who have mastered twitchin' can actually work the lure in place right next to cover until a finicky pike or muskie just can't stand it any longer. Some might argue that classic muskie jerkbaits would be equally effective here, but twitchin' experts beg to differ. Jerkbaits do indeed take plenty of big fish, but the additional vibration and built-in action of a minnow plug makes it more versatile overall. It basically does everything a jerkbait does and more.

Nearly all minnow plugs in the 5- to 7-inch range will work with this twitchin' method, but some perform better than others. Flat-sided lures have superior flash and action, attracting more strikes. The vast majority of minnow plugs available today are either wood or plastic. Wood models surely take plenty of fish, but they don't hold up under punishment. Plastic models usually produce equally well and definitely hold up a lot better.

Twitchin' a minnow plug in windy areas with a small amount of slack line enables the bait to stay in place for a long time. This is deadly for finicky, cold-front pike and muskies. Wind and wave action complement this system by washing the lure right back into the fish's lair. The lure can be twitched a few times and then paused to allow time for it to drift back over the hotspot. Sometimes, several attempts have to be made over the same spot in order to draw a strike.

Minnow bait colors should have a lot of flash. Dull colors rarely work as well. Silver, chartreuse, pearl and white patterns are all good. The "fire tiger" finish, which is a combination of chartreuse, lime and orange, is particularly good in stained waters. Flashy pearl, white or silver, which imitate shiners, ciscoes and suckers, are great in clearer lakes. Avoid using real heavy wire leaders with bulky snaps and swivels in front of any minnow bait because they severely restrict the bait's movement. Your success rate will surely suffer if you use this kind of terminal tackle. Instead, fish with a thin wire leader, or tie it directly to a small snap or preattached split ring, and use a tough, abrasion resistant line. Rarely will a pike or muskie bite off a minnow bait tied this way. Usually, nine fish out of 10 will take the lure sideways, reducing the odds of a bite-off. The minnow bait's bulk reduces the chances of the line getting near those dangerous teeth.

Twitchin' minnow baits is now a classic technique for shallow, tough-to-trigger pike and muskies. Any experienced pike or muskie chaser usually has a tackle box full of these shallow-running killers. Never underestimate them as "trigger baits." They'll come through when all else fails.

Spinnerbait Secrets

Catching pike and muskies on spinnerbaits is no big secret. Yet, few fishermen really take full advantage of a spinnerbait's versatility. While it's true that spinnerbaits are great when retrieved quickly over thick, weedy cover, they also have some deep-water applications, as well.

One of the most productive spinnerbait tactics involves allowing it to flutter downward along deep weedlines and into pockets between weed clumps. This "change up" retrieve tactic drops the spinnerbait directly in front of a big fish holding tight to deep cover. Usually, even the finickiest fish find it hard to resist such an easy prey. They simply open their big jaws and inhale it.

Pike and muskies cruising shallow reed flats are perfect targets for spinnerbaits. The single-hook design enables these lures to slip through even the thickest clumps, without hanging up. Whenever pike or muskies part the reeds as they approach a spinnerbait but are reluctant to hit, try the "change up" trick. Any sudden, sideways line movement, or a telltale "bonk" indicates a strike. In nearly every case, the spinnerbait will be lodged deeply in the corner of its mouth.

When cover isn't too thick, adding another "stinger hook"

Here's some good news for bass fishermen who go after pike: Bass spinnerbaits are just as good for pike as they are for bass. These spinnerbaits are gaining in popularity for taking pike like this.

will help you hook more fish. Pike and muskies will often swipe at a spinnerbait without ever opening their mouths. A "stinger hook" will help get these rascals. Attach the stinger upside down and your hookups will increase even more so. However, some cover situations restrict the use of a reverse stinger.

Certain spinnerbaits flutter much better than others. Balance between the leadhead, wire arm length and the style of spinner blade used critical. Usually, ½- to 1-ounce models with a short overhead wire arm and a small blade flutter are best. Long blades, such as willow leaves, are great for straight retrieves. They provide outstanding flash; however, they don't flutter well. Rounder Colorado- and Indiana-style blades are better choices here. Mounting them on a ball-bearing swivel helps even more.

Single spins (spinnerbaits with only one blade) also flutter

Adding a reverse stinger hook to your spinnerbait can greatly increase the bait's effectiveness, especially when a pike or a muskie bumps the lure with its closed mouth.

downward more rhythmically than those with two blades. Tandems provide superior lift and flash, making them excellent for shallow, straight retrieves. The less popular single spin is often the choice of professionals, however. Its versatility is unmatched. It works well on straight retrieves, but can be suddenly stopped and fluttered into a pocket or deep edge.

Color preferences differ slightly between pike and muskies. Pike will take a wider range of colors, and prefer lighter, more flashy spinner blades and skirts than muskies. For example, white spinnerbaits with hammered nickel blades are deadly on clearwater pike, while black spinnerbaits, with the same blade and just hints of white in the form of pork or plastic grubs, are more appropriate for muskies. In darker waters, yellow and hot orange work well. Once the fish's location is defined, try a number of color schemes until you find the one the fish prefer.

Straight Shaft Spinner Tips

Surprisingly, even though tons of pike and muskies are caught each year on straight-shaft spinners, few anglers really study retrieve techniques for this lure. With a little extra attention, you can make this super fish-catcher even more deadly. Perhaps the biggest improvement involves a technique called "synchro casting." What this actually refers to is how you engage your reel to start the actual retrieve. Typically, a right-handed baitcaster will pitch out a spinner, let it hit the water, and then switch the rod into the left hand for the retrieve. During this hand switch, however, the lure is momentarily allowed to sink before the actual retrieve takes place. This hesitation often results in weed-fouled lures and wasted casts. In addition, it destroys a very important strike-triggering mechanism. Because most strikes occur within the first 10 feet of a retrieve with spinners, it is more productive to start the blade spinning as soon as the lure hits the water. To accomplish this, switch your cast/retrieve hands while the spinner is in the air and engage the reel before it hits the water to begin the retrieve. This synchro-casting approach insures that the spinner has very little chance of fouling in weeds.

Long rods make spinner fishing more enjoyable than fishing them on traditional "pool cues." Instead of trying to cast a lightweight spinner on a short stick, try casting the same lure on a 7- to 7½-footer. Casting distance and efficiency is immediately increased. It also makes it much easier to figure eight a spinner at boatside, which is extremely important when muskie fishing. Four out of 10 muskies will be boated on a bucktail spinner during a *properly done* figure eight. A long rod will help you produce a deeper, longer, more controlled figure eight, and consequently increases your boatside strike percentages. A long rod will also make "bulging" a spinner over high weedtops much easier. Hold a 7½-foot rod high over your head and crank up the speed on a big-blade spinner. Presto, it's bulging *just below* the surface in a matter of seconds.

Finally, don't be afraid to really "put the pedal to the metal" with your spinner retrieve during late summer. Especially when fishing in clear-water conditions. On the other hand, if it appears that the fish are consistently striking short, slow down. This is especially true in darker waters.

Blade styles and sizes on straight-shaft spinners are always worth a close examination. Sometimes pike and muskies can be very blade conscious. Basically, large round blades make the lure lift quickly—a better choice for heavy cover and real shallow waters. Smaller, thinner blades have less water resistance and consequently run deeper. Spinners with smaller blades are better choices when extra depth is desired, or fish are not rising up to crack a shallow-running, big-bladed model.

Blade tones and colors can make a difference at times, too. Copper, brass and golds are best in coffee-stained waters. Silver, nickel, chrome and prisms are most productive in clearer lakes. Fluorescent blades really take fish in darkly stained lakes, or in any waters with a heavy algae bloom or runoff.

Straight-shaft spinners have always been great shallow-water pike and muskie producers. Big bucktail spinners are, year-in and year-out, the No. 1 muskie catchers. Both small, medium and large spinners take pike of all sizes worldwide. If you're serious about pike or muskies, spinners are a must.

Jerkbaits: Big Baits For Big Fish

There are a number of ways to take pike and muskies in shallow waters, but no technique or bait is as strange as "jerkbaits." Jerkbaits, which are more traditional muskie lures that catch lots of pike "by accident," are large wooden lures that usually have little or no inherent action. Their fish-triggering movements are created by the angler jerking a stiff-action rod.

Jerkbait anglers are a special breed unto themselves. They usually own just about every style of jerkbait made, and use them nearly all the time, no matter what the conditions may be. You could say they're hung up on one bait style, but they would surely disagree, claiming that the lure is simply better than any other most of the time.

Physically, a jerkbait fisherman usually has a strong upper body, but new, powerful lightweight rods, combined with good technique, enable just about anyone to fish jerkbaits comfortably and effectively. In fact, the tackle needed to fish jerkbaits is one of the keys to correctly working these lures, no matter who the angler is.

Short, stout 5½- to 6-foot, fast-taper rods are standard equip-

Big wooden jerkbaits are great pike and muskie baits. However, it can be difficult to hook fish consistently with them unless you have stiff tackle and very sharp hooks.

ment. New lightweight graphites are a big advantage here. They simply make it much easier to work these lures for longer periods of time, and even increase the numbers of jerking techniques. Traditional fiberglass jerkbait rods with metal reel seats fatigue the angler in short order, plus their heavy weights limit speed and technique. If you're going to do any amount of jerkbait fishing, a new lightweight graphite rod is worth its weight in gold.

A heavyweight, low-stretch line is an integral part of a jerkbait fishermen's tackle, also. Lines with a lot of stretch absorb most of the jerking motion created at the rodtip. Low-stretch lines transmit more of the rod action to the lure. Heavier-rated lines do not fatigue at the knot from casting jerkbaits, which often weigh 4 to 8 ounces. Casting these heavyweight lures and the constant jerking action quickly wears out light line. Most veteran jerkbait casters are partial to a braided dacron in the 30- to 40-pound test range. Braided dacron has very low stretch; therefore, it's the traditional favorite. New copolymer lines in the 40- to 50-pound class have similar low-stretch qualities, plus superior durability and shock strength. They also make great jerkbait lines.

Buoyant jerkbaits with a pronounced up and down action are

Double split-ringing the hooks is a good idea if you're after big fish like this one. It provides insurance that the split ring won't fail during the battle.

Shallow Water Techniques

preferred when fishing weeds that grow near the surface. They can be jerked down until they hit the weedtops, then they will float upward during line pickup. This automatically frees the lure from fouling and puts it in perfect position for the next jerk.

Manipulating the rodtip between short and long jerking motions provides the necessary depth needed for the jerkbait to constantly bump and rise through cover.

When the water gets colder in the fall, a slower rising jerkbait is desirable. Jerkbait fanatics will drill holes in their favorite wooden lures and add weight to them to decrease buoyancy. Some others will simply soak a wood jerkbait in a bucket of water or livewell to lower its buoyancy. A few even wrap lead tape around the hook shafts. All these options work.

Another style of jerkbait that can be much easier to work, and is an exceptional cold-water fish catcher as well, is the neutrally buoyant "glider" jerkbait. This lure is usually torpedo-shaped and has more of a classic side-to-side lateral action than an up-and-down movement. It is not as good in heavy weed cover, but works great around low weeds, wood and big boulders. It is usually heavier than buoyant jerkbaits, but easier to work through the water after the cast is made. A combination of simple twitches with slow, easy pulls is usually all that is needed to make this bait do its "dance."

The classic time to fish jerkbaits is when pike or muskies are not responding to "chase lures," such as spinners or shallow-running crankbaits. These fish are usually holding tight to cover, and need a strong, strike-triggering action combined with a pause that allows the fish time to react. Bumping the jerkbat into cover triggers the fish's interest, and the ensuing pause gives it the opportunity to grab the bait.

Sometimes, hooking fish on jerkbaits can be difficult because they're often made of soft wood and contain heavy hooks. Pike and muskies sink their big teeth solidly into soft woods, restricting the bait's movement during hookset. To remedy this problem, some jerkbait fishermen dip their lures in clear epoxy to prevent this from happening. Many also replace heavy hooks with thinner gauge models, and sharpen them to razor perfection.

Trolling jerkbaits is a tactic that is incredibly effective at times, but rarely used. This technique can be used to quickly cover a huge weed flat, a long rock wall or a series of small humps. It's also a good way to trigger big fish that stubbornly follow casted jerkbaits. A tired "jerkbaiter" can still work his favorite lure after a long day on the water by trolling late in the afternoon. (A good angler needs to explore his options and try different techniques.)

Jerkbaits are traditional favorites of muskie fishermen, but are equally good pike lures. It's always a good idea to try one when either one of these fish is hesitant to chase a spinner or free-swimming crankbait. Jerkbaits create a strong, strike-triggering response, and have a big-bait/big-fish appeal that's unlike any other lure, especially in shallow waters.

10

Deep-Water Tactics

S ome muskie and pike fishermen don't believe that good deep-water tactics exist. However, there are a number of ways to locate and catch deep-water pike and muskies, but none of them work in every fishing situation. One thing that must be considered when fishing deep water is that the fish will be scattered and may not be actively feeding. Although it's not true in every case, deep-water pike and muskies are often in a negative mode, making them difficult to catch even when you locate them. Some anglers also pass up deep-water fish because they feel the excitement doesn't compare to the lure-smashing, heart-thumping thrill that comes when a shallow-water fish strikes at boatside.

In defense of deep-water fishing, it must be noted that anglers have caught many huge fish (including muskies weighing more than 50 pounds) while deep-water trolling. In fact, some of the old muskie hunters say the only way to catch a really big fish is to ply the depths.

Planer Boards And Downriggers

Muskies and pike head for deep-water haunts for various reasons. Weather conditions, water temperatures, food availability and fishing pressure can all play roles singly or in combination. Successful trollers have ways of dredging up those deep-water fish, however. They use multiple rods, where legal, and run a variety of lures into the strike zone with planer boards and downriggers. Pike

This nice string of northerns, along with a "bonus" walleye, was taken in deep water with the use of a slow presentation of dead bait and quick-set rigs.

Deep-Water Tactics

and muskie hunters have successfully borrowed these trolling devices from Great Lakes salmon trollers. Downriggers allow precise depth control, while planer boards spread lures over a wide area.

Sometimes, there's no telling where muskies and pike will hold. They'll often stage off feeding areas, holding in 25 to 40 feet of water some distance away from a rock bar, rock pile or submerged hump. They may even suspend only a few feet down in deep water, 100 or more feet from the structure. In any case, begin your efforts near structure where muskies and pike might feed, and expand your search from there, using sonar, downriggers, planer boards or both as the situation dictates.

With the use of a mast that mounts near the bow, large planer boards can be run a great distance off to the side of the boat. Smaller boards can be run inside the longer boards. Add downriggers to the formula and a team of three anglers can troll a wide swath at varying depths. When fishing multiple rigs, however, make sure you check load regulations. Some states allow only one rod per angler.

When a likely piece of structure has been located, such as an underwater hump, the tactic is to set the two outside lines about 80 feet out to each side with lures running 5 to 7 feet below the surface. The inside planer boards, set halfway between the boat and outside boards, should pull lures which are running closer to the boat; this can be in the 12- to 15-foot range. Set the downriggers to run in the 20- to 25-foot range.

Once everything is rigged, it's a simple matter of trolling in circles around the submerged hump. Make the initial circle fairly close to the hump, with each additional circle being a bit farther out. Systematically search the entire area. If you fail to connect with a predator, try again with the lures set at different depths. Drop the outer lures 8 to 10 feet, the inside 20 to 25 feet, and, the downriggers 30 to 35 feet. Resume the trolling search around the structure. This type of trolling can work on various types of structure. It's just a matter of using a depthfinder to help keep you on the right track and to ensure that the lures are running at the proper depths.

Trolling in this manner requires a lot of gear and even more "know how." Each angler has to know the routine when that trophy fish strikes. Empty lines and downriggers must be reeled in while boat control is maintained. Only after the extra lines are in

Complete Angler's Library

Multi-Rig Trolling Pattern

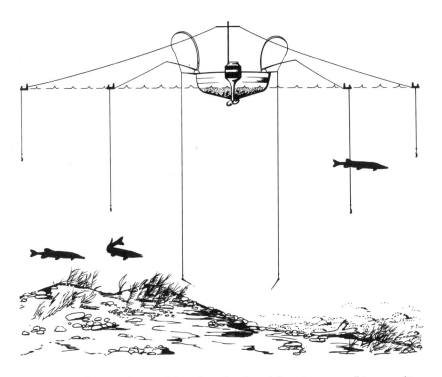

This drawing illustrates the use of skis, planer boards and downriggers to troll in a searching pattern along a hump. This puts the baits at various depths while searching for pike or muskies.

can the boat be stopped. The whole process resembles a mine sweeping operation—the real fun begins when you find what you're looking for.

Crankbaits And Wire Line

Trolling over, around and through schools of suspended baitfish is also effective when it comes to locating deep-water pike and muskies. Once again, the angler should use a flasher, graph or LCD to find schools of suspended forage fish, and to determine how deep to run the lures. Downriggers aren't the only solution for deep-water predators, however. Deep-diving crankbaits are excellent for working depths of 15 to 35 feet. If you use wire or lead-core line, you can work at even greater depths. There is no doubt that deep-diving lures work. Muskie legend Len Hartman made history with his crankbaits—three muskies over 60 pounds (each is quite a testimonial in itself).

The drawback to these giant deep-divers is that you need arms like an Olympic weightlifter if you plan on trolling for more than a few hours. A set of high-quality rod holders can be invaluable in this situation. They make deep-water trolling more comfortable and fun, extending the hours you're willing to devote to trolling.

In most cases, the boat's forward movement will even set the hooks. Of course the hooks must be honed to perfect sharpness so the barbs will penetrate a muskie's or pike's bony mouth.

Wire line is the choice when the fish are holding deeper than the trolling lures will reach. Deep-water weedbeds or the deep edges of shallow weedbeds are perfect examples of this type of situation. Using a depthfinder, you can maintain trolling position along the edge, and allow the wire to take the lure to the proper depth. Another advantage wire line has over monofilament is that it will slice through vegetation. If you're line is caught in vegetation, you need only give a good jerk or two on the rod. You don't have to reel it in. This saves time and energy.

If wire-lining doesn't suit you, a simple three-way swivel, rigged with a heavy sinker at the end of a 6-inch dropline, will sometimes suffice. The three-way rig works much like a downrigger, except that you'll have to fight the sinker's weight, as well as the fish. Normally, you'll fish a three-way rig in the 20- or 30-foot depths. The 4 to 8 ounces required to sink a small lure to the desired trolling depth is not enough to hinder an angler who is using heavy tackle.

Late fall is prime time for using a three-way rig to take trophy northerns. Weather transitions and falling water temperatures push pike into deeper water. The fish will be feeding, but you'll have to reduce trolling speed and run the bait right over them. Baits such as Fat Raps, Rat-L-Traps, Rattlin' Raps or No. 13 Floating Rapalas often work best. Colors such as chartreuse, fluorescent orange, bright yellow or combinations of these colors really turn on late-fall pike.

Open-Water Fishing

Heavy fishing pressure often drives pike and muskies into open water. In their efforts to escape anglers, who often thrash the surface into a froth with huge lures, they'll swim out into deeper water where they'll suspend 10 or 15 feet down. What happens, at times, is that they'll simply move out from their shallow-water haunts but remain at the same depth. A few anglers have figured out this phenomenon and found success. It's just a matter of trolling a variety of baits at different depths. It can be a hit-or-miss operation, but one that often does produce fish.

Predators Love Real Meat

Deep-water pike and muskies sometimes turn off, and start ignoring fast-moving artificials. Smart anglers take the hint and switch to real baitfish. Fished slowly, live or dead bait is a tantalizing, easy-to-catch meal. During the summer months, live bait usually out-performs dead fare—for both pike and muskies. Fish the live bait around those rock piles or bars in 35 to 40 feet of water. Start by plotting the structure with your depthfinder, marking the edges and shallowest point with marker buoys. Then, search every nook and cranny around the edges, and don't forget the top.

The old adage of big bait catches big fish is true. Chubs 10 to 12 inches long are just right. If the cover isn't too heavy, the best hooking system going is a quick-set rig. This twin-hook system, with one stationary hook and one that can slide along the leader, allows you to set the hook the instant a fish takes the bait. Hooking ratios climb, while the number of deep-hooked fish falls. Quick-set rigs almost ensure that the fish will be hooked in the mouth, making it possible to release the fish unharmed. As soon as a strike occurs, it becomes a matter of tightening the line and setting the hooks.

Live bait in numerous ways can be presented with a quick-set rig. One is to put enough weight ahead of the leader to sink the bait to the bottom. While watching the depthfinder and following the preset marker buoys, use your electric trolling motor to slowly troll the bait along the bottom. Stop here and there, allowing the bait to rest each spot for a short time. Start by working the bait across the top of the structure, then along the edges and finally into the surrounding deeper water.

Every few feet, slowly lift the rodtip about 3 feet, then allow the bait to fall back to the bottom where it remains motionless for about 30 seconds before moving on. When a fish strikes, point the rodtip at the fish and set the hooks hard when the line tightens.

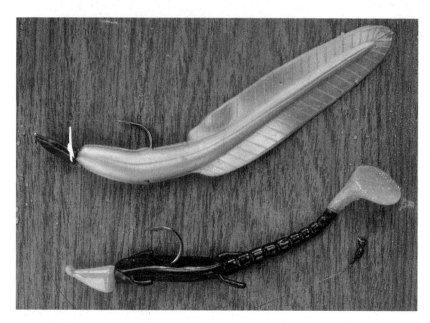

These popular muskie-pike jig setups are particularly effective in deep-water jigging situations. For extra hooking power, try adding a "stinger" hook to the jig.

Suspending live bait over deep-water structure with a slip bobber is another productive method. A live chub suspended a couple of feet above the bottom, over a deep-water rock pile, can be extremely effective at taking big muskies or pike, especially when the predators are not actively feeding. Once again, offer this presentation with a quick-set rig. With a slip bobber, you can set the quick-set rig at any depth. The large, European-style slip bobbers, made of balsa wood, are perfect for this kind of use. They can easily support up to a pound of weight.

Deep-Water Jigging

Vertical jigging has proved to be a solid and sound fishing method for walleyes, but knowledgeable pike and muskie hunters also know that this method works on their favorite fish. The techniques are basically identical, except for the size of the bait presented. All you need is some heavyweight jig heads, in the 2- to 6-ounce range, with large, stout hooks. Six inches of uncoated wire, at least 30-pound test, should be used to attach a stinger hook to the jig. Use a No. 2 treble for the stinger. Either live or dead bait works well on the jig-and-stinger combination.

The most productive jigging spots are rock bars, humps, rock piles or the ends of deep-water points. Experienced anglers, using a depthfinder or graph, can even locate and catch suspended deep-water pike and muskies. Simply lower the jig (you can see it on a flasher screen) to the fish. Remember, however, that most fish like to swim up to a target from below. When jigging, rely on the lift and fall to attract the fish, but be ready for a strike on the fall. Lift the jig 3 or 4 feet and let it drop. Twitch the rodtip a few times, then let it rest about a minute. Follow with a shorter lift, about a foot; let it fall, twitch and rest again. Repeat the process until you connect with your trophy.

The strike, when it comes, can be vicious, but more often it is very subtle. Even huge muskies and pike can take a bait without the angler feeling a thing. Stay alert and keep a sharp eye on the line. If it twitches or if the lure seems to stop falling, set the hook.

Fishing the deep water for big muskies and pike is foreign to a lot of anglers, but the trophy fish are there if you just take the time to look.

Special Situations

11

Early-Spring
Dead-Baiting Pike

Larger fish usually exhibit traits that differ from the rest of their species. They live in different areas, feed at different times and often eat entirely different foods. However, the northern pike is an especially "strange brew" in this respect. Huge populations of small- to mid-sized pike are nearly always aggressive. They'll ravage nearly anything that swims on the surface or beneath, no matter if it's spring, summer or fall. A cover of ice doesn't seem to slow them down either. They are feeding machines with super-cranked metabolisms. Yet, once they reach trophy size it's like they become different fish.

How different? Pike over 40 inches long avoid warmer waters preferred by their smaller cousins. They seek out ice-cold pockets of deep water far removed from other small- to mid-ranged pike. And, they are rarely as aggressive as smaller pike. Big pike are more apt to take a slow-moving jig or vertically worked spoon than chase down a fast-whirling spinner.

But, perhaps the most unusual phenomena is how dead bait appeals to a big pike. No, this is not a misprint—big pike love dead bait. A lively wiggling shiner minnow fished off a tip-up through the ice is sure to catch loads of pike. However, a dead, slimy smelt hung off a weird-looking v-shaped hook is more apt to tempt a lunker. There's no argument that this statement sounds crazy, but there's more truth to it than most pike anglers suspect, though many are starting to catch on.

Surprisingly, muskies do not share the pike's fondness for dead

These river pike are proof that the early-spring, dead-baiting tactic works, and works well. These northerns were taken at the mouth of a feeder stream entering the river.

Early-Spring Dead-Baiting Pike   151

bait. Undoubtedly, a few have been caught on the rigs we are about to describe, but muskie hunters will find other baits and lures much more effective.

Why big pike in particular like dead bait is still a mystery. However, when both live bait and dead bait are fished side by side, the dead bait usually takes the bigger fish. This is especially true in cold waters of spring, fall and winter. Some of the world's best pike anglers have extensively tested live bait against dead in a variety of situations in order to determine "why." Their theories might surprise you.

For example, a group of anglers fishing a well-known pike spawning run that annually takes place in the backbays of the famed Missouri River reservoirs, Lakes Oahe and Sakakawea, rigged lively minnows on bobbers and fished them side by side with dead-bait setups. Surprisingly, dead bait was the best big-pike producer throughout the entire spring spawning run. Others have made similar tests and the results are always the same: The majority of big pike take the dead bait rigs.

Many ice fishermen claim the same results. Big-pike ice fishing specialists from the heavily fished waters near large cities such as Minneapolis, Chicago, Milwaukee, New York and Winnipeg to the remote Canadian wilderness waters agree that dangling dead bait off a tip-up is far more effective for lunkers than a lively minnow. The lively minnow takes plenty of pike, but the trophies consistently fall for the dead one.

One theory is that the pike's metabolism, much like ours, makes drastic changes as it gets older. As it matures, its sense of smell improves, as well. It becomes less dependent on sight feeding and chasing down fast-moving prey. Instead, it masters opportunistic feeding. Easy-to-get food becomes the norm. Slow swimming prey that is 10 to 20 percent of the pike's body weight becomes its normal target. Big suckers, redhorse, bullheads, burbot and carp are typical tablefare. This makes a lot of sense, and is probably a partial answer to the dead-bait question.

Being opportunistic feeders with a superior sense of smell, big pike will slowly move along the bottom scavenging dead bait. In some cases, such as just after ice-out, food availability can be scarce. This is also a time when die-offs of minnows and other fish occur in small creeks and bays. These small fish were either trapped during ice breakup or were victims of low-oxygen levels

Here's a bait all rigged up and ready to use for enticing northerns into attacking. The smell of dead bait is irresistible to pike when the ice is just leaving the lake.

prior to the spring thaw. The smell of dead bait in these areas attracts big pike which slowly scavenge the terrain as they move into suitable spawning waters.

High-protein forage such as smelt are highly sought after by big pike, also. Smelt populations flourish in many of the Great Lakes and several big inland pike waters. Pike follow them into creeks and small rivers each spring. Smelt are very soft-bodied, delicate minnows. They die easily, especially during their massive movements in to propagate. It's a sure thing that bigger pike slowly cruise the creek bottom in search of dead smelt during this time. Perhaps this is one of the reasons why dead smelt, in particular, are such a great choice for dead-bait fishing.

Smelt are not the only dead bait that work for pike, however. Dead suckers, shiners, herring, ciscoes and whitefish all take big pike. Some anglers actually prefer one of these other minnow species over smelt, usually because of size. Rarely do smelt grow much larger than 7 inches. Some big-pike specialists simply want bigger baits. Two of the most popular dead baits in the Midwest for ice fishing are bloaters (large herring) or dead suckers in the 8- to 15-inch range. Pike have always had a special place in their jaws for sucker minnows, and they don't seem to mind if the minnows are alive or dead.

European pike angling authority Fred Buller firmly believes in this shift in a pike's nature during its life. In fact, he's gone as far as to categorize the feeding behavior of lunker pike. Buller believes a big pike's first preference is to scavenge dead bait. He also believes, as do others, that lunker pike have honed this skill in order to obtain maximum nutrition with little expended energy.

According to Buller, the pike's second choice is to capitalize on injured prey. His belief that all highly efficient predators, even mammals such as wolves and coyotes, scavenge whenever possible, and attack injured prey as their second most efficient means of feeding. Buller thinks that the bigger pike prefer to ambush live, uninjured prey only as a third option. However, their preference in live food is somewhat specific at times. Large, slow-moving forage that are 10 to 20 percent of a pike's weight is most acceptable. Once more, minimal energy is expended chasing down the prey, while the size provides maximum nourishment.

A big pike's attraction to dead bait is nothing new to ardent pike chasers. But, to some anglers, it comes as quite a shock. However, once you realize why a trophy-class pike prefers dead bait, you begin to put the whole picture together. It makes a lot of sense when comparisons to predators like wolves and coyotes are drawn. After all, *Esox lucius* really means "water wolf."

Dead-Bait Rigs

An almost endless array of dead-bait rigs are available for pike fishing. Some contain unusual amounts of hardware and strange hook designs, while others are almost ultra-light by comparison. All of these rigs have produced big pike over the years. Some are better tailored for ice fishing, while others are more suited for open water. Let's take a look at several of the most popular dead-bait rigs.

The famous Swedish hook has been around for a long time. It

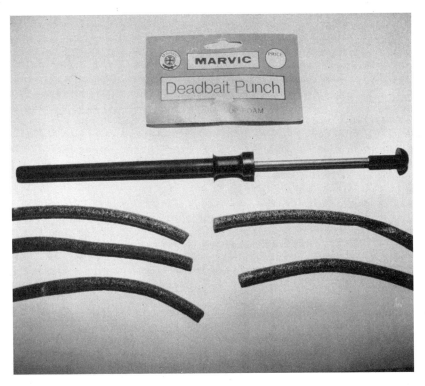

A dead-bait punch is a handy tool to have in your tackle box when using a dead-bait presentation for pike. The tool (top) is inserted into the mouth of the baitfish and forced inside the fish. This creates a path for Styrofoam injection into the body cavity. The bait then floats off the bottom, giving the pike a better chance to attack it. How high the bait floats depends upon the amount of Styrofoam that is injected.

was developed originally for ice fishing in order to present a dead bait, such as a big smelt minnow, in a horizontal position. As odd as this hook looks at first glance, it is easy to work with and it hooks pike very well.

Rig a smelt on the Swedish hook by inserting the hook in the dorsal fin or anal area of the smelt. Then, when the threading portion reaches the hook bend, pull back on it while pressing against the back of the minnow with your thumb. This will pop the hook point out. It's now ready to fish.

Tying a heavyweight monofilament leader to the Swedish hook is perfectly acceptable. Rarely do pike inhale the rig beyond the large overhead wire arm. However, some pike purists scorn this practice, preferring to attach a wire leader to reduce any chance of a bite-off.

When a pike strikes this rig, the hook must be set during the initial run. The hook is immediately in position so there's no need to wait. But, what's even more important is that a pike cannot swallow this rig easily, so it will disgorge it after that first run-out. The big overhead wire arm is too much for the pike to swallow. This, of course, protects the fish from serious injury. Many pike lovers prefer the Swedish hook for this reason alone. Plenty of pike can be caught without seriously injuring them.

Strong tackle and a solid hookset are essential with the Swedish hook setup. This is not for the ultra-light enthusiast or the guy who likes to play his fish. Muscle is the key word here. Heavyweight line in the 40- to 50-pound range is recommended. Stay close to your tip-ups, and get to the "flag" right away. Pull the tip-up out while the pike is still running, snub the line with your hand and jerk solidly upward. Continue to maintain strong, even pressure throughout the battle or the hook will dislodge.

A modified version of the Swedish hook was developed in Wisconsin. It's called the Flagel Rig, and it incorporates a separate piece of wire to keep the dead bait hanging horizontally. An independent wire leader and treble hook is then attached to a loop in the wire form and to the dead bait. This idea works well because the added leverage provided by the rigid, heavy Swedish hook is eliminated. Any number of hooking combinations can be used with this rig successfully.

Another unique dead-bait hook is Mustad's universal double bait hook. It is commonly used all across the Scandinavian countries for smelt fishing. In the U.S., it is marketed with an attached wire leader and called "The Missouri River Pike Rig." What's great about this hook is that it has a needle-like head that can be easily detached from the rig, threaded through the dead smelt and then reattached to the leader. It makes rigging dead smelt a snap. The twin hooks on this rig feature a nice deep bend with excellent hook points. They penetrate quickly and solidly. This is an excellent dead-bait rig.

On the other side of the spectrum are the newer thin-gauge, quick-set rigs for dead-bait fishing. These rigs feature thin wire leaders and a series of smaller hooks. Several different hook styles are used and all seem to work well. The European VB hook is less popular in the U.S. and Canada, but highly touted by professionals who have used it. It features a small live-bait hook welded on

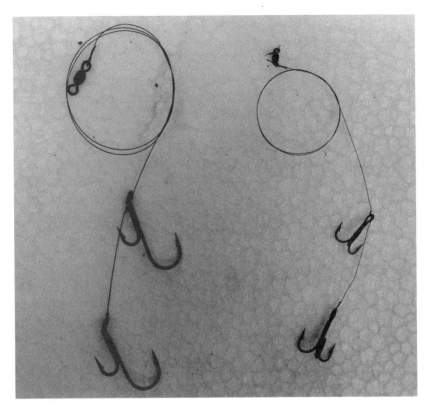

These rigs represent a slight variation of the quick-set rigs diagrammed on page 71. The rig at left incorporates European VB hooks while the one at right has two small, needle-sharp trebles. Both work well with dead bait.

the opposite side of a medium-sized, single hook. The larger hook has a superior temper compared to standard hooks of this size, and the barbs are much sharper. The small hook is anchored in the dead bait, while the large one protrudes openly on the opposite side. Most Europeans fish this setup off spinning gear.

Quick-set rigs made with small, needle-sharp trebles work extremely well, too. The most popular hook sizes are No. 6 and No. 4, but occasionally smaller or larger sizes are used. The tiny trebles set easily into any size pike, and hold securely as long as the angler doesn't exert too much force. These treble version quick-set rigs are best fished with lighter tackle, also. The lighter gear prevents anglers from over-pressuring the fish during battle.

Quick-set rigs can be fished in a variety of situations. While they work well on live and dead bait, they might need a special harness for dead-bait fishing if the angler wants to suspend his bait horizontally. A wire form similar to the one used on the Flagel Rig can be easily adapted for quick-set rigs. The wire form holds the bait upright, while the rig is anchored.

In open-water applications, quick-set rigs can be still-fished on the bottom with or without weight, or off any number of bobber/float setups. No matter how it's fished, however, casting is *not* recommended. Most dead bait simply will not hold up to continued casting. On top of that, the fish are not as responsive to it. One long cast to spot is acceptable. At that point, a waiting game combined with very little bait movement is most desirable.

Europeans do more shore-fishing for big pike than North Americans. They have devised some outstanding shore-fishing concepts both in the bait rigs and equipment used. One of their most popular shore-fishing setups, the Paternoster Rig, is particularly good. A large bell sinker-style weight anchors the very end of the Paternoster Rig. This added weight makes it easy to cast and enables the shore fishermen to suspend one or more dead baits in between. The Missouri River Pike Rig basically employs the same tail sinker concept.

Strike indicators are an important part of all dead-bait fishing. Ice fishermen rely on a tip-up flag, which works very well. Shore fishermen commonly use a clicker device on their baitcasting reels or a visible sign, such as some attachment to the line, just above the tip-top. Many Europeans prefer spinning equipment anchored to extra long 10- to 20-foot rods for shore-fishing. They open the reel's bail and attach the line to a small hairpin or paper clip, along with attaching in the same area a small paper or cloth flag as a bite indicator. When a strike occurs, the line is pulled from the clip, allowing the pike to take line. At the same time, the small flag drops, letting the angler know what's happening.

Still others utilize bobbers/floats as bite indicators, even when bottomfishing. The float keeps the majority of the line up near the surface, allowing the angler to closely monitor the movements of a pike after the strike. These are often called "pilot floats" by Europeans. The concept works quite well.

Best Early-Spring Pike Spots

The best early-spring pike spots are not hard to find. They all have some commonly recognizable features. In fact, just before

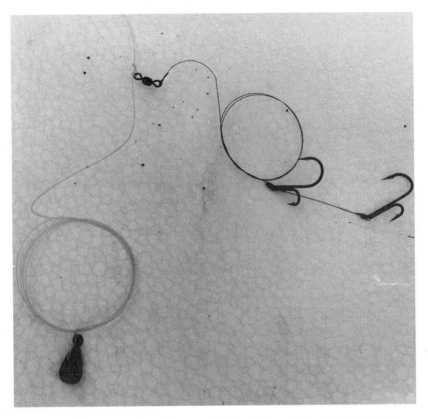

Called the Paternoster Rig, this setup is great for shore-fishing with dead bait. The bait is suspended between rodtip and weight. Strikes are easily detected, and hookset is quick.

ice-out, these spots usually stand out like a sore thumb. They are small, open-water spots in an otherwise frozen scene. This could be an incoming creek or small river, but it might also be nothing more than a sun-exposed marsh on the northern end of the lake. In reservoirs, small secluded bays and feeder cuts receiving lots of early-spring sunlight are ideal. The best spots in clear lakes and reservoirs have slightly off-colored water. All of these spots attract big pike preparing to spawn.

Some of the best early-spring pike exist in large river systems. The St. Lawrence, Mississippi, Missouri and Wisconsin rivers all produce 20-pound pike each spring. Smaller rivers in Canada such as the McKenzie and Churchill are also hotbeds. Alaska has some premier big-pike rivers, such as the Notak, Yukon and Tanana, that are virtually untapped. The endless array of rivers and creeks

In the spring, the sight of this creek mouth should start a pike or muskie angler's adrenalin pumping. This is a prime spot for dead-baiting pike, and later on you'll find muskies here, too.

that dump into the Great Lakes all carry potential, some more than others.

Small bays off these rivers that contain marshy lowlands are hotspots. The key is to pinpoint an area that pike frequently pass in numbers. Experimenting at first is a must. Try several spots until some success is achieved. Then close in on the best "spot on the spot." Analyze the producing area more closely. Some unique feature will be the pike producer time and time again. It's simply a matter of finding it.

Creek mouths off a large river have tremendous potential. When angling pressure is not an issue, shore-fishing is very productive. Set up dead-bait rigs inside any slack-water areas near current. The best big-pike spot, percentagewise, around creek mouths is the small, deep hole where the creek dumps into the main river. If the area is a popular fishing spot, anchor where you can still precisely present a number of still-fishing rigs to the potential hotspots where the largest pike will most likely be found, laying in wait for an easy meal.

Dead bait's effectiveness on big pike is becoming known worldwide. What seems like a strange phenomenon to some anglers is easily accepted by others (especially true of the Europeans who have been taking advantage of it much longer than North Americans).

If you truly want a legitimate shot at a real big pike this coming year, still-fishing dead bait in the early spring or wintertime might be your best bet. Big pike are the most susceptible at those times of the year. And, they seem to have an affinity for a smelly dead bait that hardly moves. What could be more simple?

12

Nightfishing For Muskies

Until recently, few anglers were aware that muskies fed after dark. It was widely thought that muskies, just like their cousin the northern pike, were midday sight feeders rarely caught after nightfall. In fact, fish caught after dark were considered flukes. Boy, how times have changed! Articles now appear regularly about catching muskies after dark. It appears that anglers everywhere are finding out how much muskies actually feed in total darkness. What others missed out on for decades, today's anglers are now finding out about in a *big* way.

Not all lakes are good for nightfishing, however. The best nightfishing lakes for muskies are usually clear and have lots of boat traffic. The more boat traffic and fishing pressure, the better. The warm, summer months are generally more productive after dark for muskies than spring and fall. One might argue that this is water temperature related, but experienced anglers continue to have good night action into the fall on some waters. It is now believed that increased boat traffic is the biggest factor. During summer months, traffic is usually at a peak. However, if traffic picks up early in the spring or continues on into the fall, strong night movements still occur.

No matter what lake you're fishing, some degree of muskie feeding activity takes place during that final light of day. This is predictably the best time to catch big muskies. No matter how good or bad fishing is beforehand, a predictable muskie movement

Hot, muggy nights and clear lakes with a lot of boat traffic can be a combination that produces outstanding muskie action. This 33½-pounder hit a crankbait at boatside at 1:30 a.m.

Nightfishing For Muskies

always occurs right after sunset. In fact, after a severe cold front, this might be the *only* time that muskies feed. Ironically, this is usually when most anglers give up and put their boat on the trailer. Yet, it's during that "last night" that the biggest muskie movement of the day is usually taking place. This movement is totally predictable. Here's how you can capitalize on it.

Muskies on many lakes can be taken in amazingly shallow water after dark. This even includes big fish. The best shallow movements of muskies at night occur on slightly stained waters that aren't overly pressured by night traffic.

The best weapon for taking shallow-cruising night muskies is a big, black bucktail with a No. 8 Colorado blade. Large black models are preferred because they provide a bigger silhouette, making it easier for fish to zero-in on. In addition, the No. 8 Colorado blade produces a sound frequency that is apparently superior to other blades. Big spinnerbaits are also real good night baits for muskies. They produce excellent vibration and silhouettes. They can also be worked both shallow and fairly deep. In this respect, they're much more versatile than the more popular straight-shaft bucktail spinner.

Surface baits have a place in the night fisherman's arsenal, too, but they're often overused. Surface baits produce best on real warm nights with flat, calm water when fished over thick weed cover or clear, shallow bars. They are poor producers during or after cold fronts, or when any kind of wave action exists.

The best surface lures are high-noise, slow-speed versions. This eliminates a lot of choices. Most surface lures require some degree of speed to activate their best built-in action. The more speed that is needed, the poorer choice the lure is for night muskies. Creeper, wobbler or jittering-style baits are the top choices because they can be worked slowly.

Even though many muskies can be taken in the shallows after dark, few anglers realize the potential for action in deeper waters. The vast majority of muskie fishermen fish too shallow, reducing their chances for big fish. Big muskies are rarely shallow in lakes with a lot of pressure. They stay deep nearly all the time, even after dark. The best way to catch them is with jointed, deep-diving crankbaits.

When jointed deep divers wiggle through the water, they produce a unique clicking sound when the two separate body parts hit

This selection of lures works well when nightfishing for muskies. It includes (from left) a big tandem spinnerbait, a jointed Creeper and a jointed deep diver lure.

each other. This clicking sound drives muskies wild. No straight model plug produces nearly as well as a jointed version in this instance. The best deep divers work well at slow-retrieve speeds, too. A noisy, jointed deep diver coming through the water at a slow to medium speed is simply too much for active night muskies to resist.

The most productive deep-water feeding zone after dark appears to be in depths from 8 to 18 feet. Casters should concentrate heavily on large weed flats and center weed bars with noticeable signs of baitfish activity. The best weedbeds in deep, clear lakes have lots of baitfish, and are situated in unique locations such as in narrows, on or around mid-lake humps or on pronounced points or turns in otherwise featureless flats. Muskies will often bury themselves in thick weeds on these spots during daylight pe-

Nightfishing For Muskies   165

riods. They're not only disinterested in your lure presentations at this time, but most often they can't even see them. The secret here is to wait them out. Spend the least unproductive daytime hours casting and trolling these same areas with a mapping and learning attitude in mind. Then, attack them hard after dark with the increased knowledge of where points, turns, thicker clumps and pockets are located.

Other productive night crankin' areas are shallow, rocky humps or large, shallow bars with some small portions of rock on them. In gin-clear lakes with little or no weed growth, these sandbars often have sunken man-made cribs or brush piles on them. When weeds aren't present, these woody structures are key producers.

Steep banks and steep-breaking shallow points are good fall night spots. They are usually the spawning areas for cold-water baitfish such as ciscoes in deep, clear lakes. The setting sun triggers a massive movement of these silvery minnows into the shallows to spawn. And, muskies are often right there to enjoy the minnow smorgasbord.

Trollers have many more deep-water options for nightfishing. They can still work a weedline, but deeper breaklines and deeper cresting humps in the 12- to 18-foot range can be worked much more effectively. Usually, trolling doubles the running depth of a casted lure. In other words, if your favorite crankbait runs 8 feet deep when casted on 30-pound line, it will usually run 16 feet when trolled. This, of course, opens up lots of options. These same areas can be covered much deeper with a series of trolling passes. Trolling has another advantage during the fall when it gets cold. You can easily hold a trolling rod while wearing gloves, or you can simply put it in a rod holder and warm your hands any number of ways. The caster, of course, must constantly use his hands.

Rigging up with the extra-long, 9- to 10-foot rods with a limber tip and dropping down on the line size is a good idea for night trolling, too. Usually, a 20-pound test is plenty strong; yet, it allows crankbaits to run much deeper than most traditionally-used muskie lines of 30-pound test or more. The thicker-diameter, 40- to 50-pound test lines are inefficient for deep-water trolling because they severely limit the depths at which anglers can effectively run their baits.

Nightfishing is the best way to take trophy muskies in heavily traveled, clear-water lakes. Working deeper drop-offs in late fall after dark will produce big muskies.

Secondary breaklines, commonly call "the deeper drop-offs," are big muskie producers in the late fall after dark on clear lakes. Usually, these secondary breaklines are somewhere from 18 to 28 feet deep, but they can be deeper. Coincidentally, these breaklines usually correlate closely with the summer thermocline. The biggest muskies in *any* body of water will hang in this depth range—suspended just above the thermocline during the summer months, and hugging the secondary breakline in the fall. Trolling deep with additional weight on lighter line is the *only* effective way to fish them.

Other Points To Remember

Some specialized equipment is needed for night muskies. For one, good lights are a must. Most ardent night muskie hunters wear some kind of a headlamp. Several styles are available. Most of them are okay, but often their lighting power is limited. The best headlamps have a big battery unit and a Krypton bulb. With a headlamp, the night angler can quickly switch on a light after a muskie is hooked, and keep it on the fish during the battle, without having someone holding a flashlight. A headlamp also works

After you've won the battle, a good headlamp is invaluable for providing adequate light for handling the fish. Have your tools close at hand, and use a plumber's glove.

well for the person handling the landing net. Both hands are free to work the big net effectively.

All tools used for unhooking fish should be easily accessible and stored in the same place all the time. All lures not being used should be put away along with any other unnecessary gear. A clean, clutter-free boat floor is a must. Only the bare essentials for nightfishing should be accessible. A boat's running lights should be in top working order. Safety is a major concern after dark. Everyone on the water should be following the same set of rules. To make sure they are, scan the water in front of you with a high-powered spotlight when traveling between spots. This helps prevent running into another boat or hitting floating debris.

Above all, know the water well before venturing out onto it after dark. Fishing unfamiliar waters at night is not a good idea.

Hitting a shallow reef is dangerous enough during the day; after dark, it can be disastrous.

Night-feeding muskies on heavily traveled lakes is one of the biggest secrets to be uncovered in the past 15 years. Few still believe it is possible. Those that do, often fall short because they fail to fish the best potential areas or cast the right kinds of lures. Good "day spots" are also *great* "night spots." Big bucktails with round blades are the weapon for heavy weeds, but never underestimate the jointed deep diver for nearly all other situations. An allegiance to deep-diving crankbaits will pay huge dividends in bigger fish. They get down where the big ones live, and do a better job of keeping a big fish on after it is hooked.

Take this chapter seriously and you'll score on some big fish. Start concentrating more on lakes with big-fish reputations and heavy boat traffic. Big muskies are susceptible after dark, and at almost any other time, on heavily pressured lakes. Be one of the few to take full advantage of this.

=13=

Big Suckers—Fall Muskies

Staggering is the best word to describe the number of muskies caught each season on live suckers. When the water gets cold, muskies simply cannot resist properly presented lively suckers. They are a natural forage in almost all muskie waters, and the fish really key on them. What's even more impressive is the actual amount of trophy muskies over 35 pounds taken with big suckers. When the objective is catching a really big muskie in the fall, nothing does the trick quite like a big sucker. No doubt, the top professional muskie guides in northern Wisconsin are aware of the trophy potential of suckers. Six of the past 10 Wisconsin state champion muskies have been caught by anglers fishing with big suckers in the fall, and every one of those six fish weighed over 40 pounds.

These fall muskies are taken quite often in deep water. In clear lakes, deep fringes of green weed growth in the 12- to 18-foot range can be very productive. Drifting a sucker off a float or on a short free-line works well here. This is a classic way to fish suckers for muskies.

The most popular floats over the years have been 3- to 4-inch diameter, round, cork balls with holes through the centers. The line is simply pegged in the cork with a small stick. When the hook is set, this stick usually pops out, and the cork floats free, out of the way during the battle.

Big snap-on plastic bobbers are rarely used by the professionals because their biggest drawback is that they're fixed, and won't pop

Big suckers can trick some of the wariest trophies into striking. This 44½-pounder—the biggest caught in Wisconsin in 1985—took a 22-inch sucker in 35 feet of water.

free. Thus, this bobber is usually in the way when landing the fish. Plus, they're usually more buoyant than needed.

A lot of experienced sucker fishermen have recently switched to large European-style slip floats appropriately called "center sliders." These floats are basically large slip bobbers with an oval-shaped body. A small "pilot float," about the size of an ice-fishing bobber used for panfish, is attached to guide the angler in following a big fish after the strike.

On the vast majority of lakes, the best sucker-fishing areas are deep, hard-bottom breaklines, often called "secondary breaks." This is that section of water where the hard bottom meets the lake's basin of silt. Normally, this secondary break is in 18 to 38 feet of water, but it can be deeper. A log, big rock or any other irregular cover along this break is a potential fish-holding spot. Free-lining suckers along this breakline will take fish.

When severe, arctic weather hits during the fall, muskies in shallower lakes will often bunch up in small, hard-bottom holes making them extremely vulnerable. Drifting or still-fishing sucker rigs in these areas can produce awesome numbers of big fish. The few professionals who are aware of this little known phenomenon reap the big-fish benefits each and every time this weather pattern develops. This is where slow-drifting, backtrolling or still-fishing a sucker is particularly deadly because it puts an irresistible bait in front of a large number of big fish.

Single-hook rigs are traditionally preferred by many professionals because they're easy to use with large suckers. They seldom snag, and they present the big sucker in a very natural manner. But, there are some real tricks to fishing this single-hook rig effectively. One of the biggest secrets is in matching hook size to the size of the sucker. Most sucker fishermen simply use too small of a hook. The popular 8/0 to 10/0 sizes used by the majority are fine for small suckers under 15 inches, but a serious trophy fisherman wouldn't consider anything less than a 12/0. Another little-known trick the professionals use is bending out the point of a classic square sucker hook to increase its hooking ability. The large, bony head of a big sucker greatly reduces hook penetration. A muskie that has taken a sucker often disgorges the single-hook rig without ever actually having the hook penetrate. This is because the sucker's big head prevents this from happening. Bending out the hook point slightly helps eliminate this problem.

Sucker Float Rig

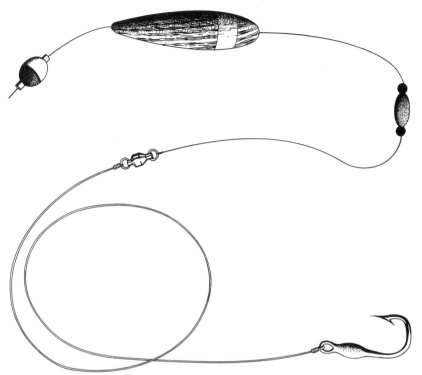

This sucker float rig is a combination of American and European live-bait techniques. It consists of a weighted sucker hook, a 36-inch wire leader, a 1-ounce rubber core sinker, a big "center-slider" float, a bobber stop and a pilot float.

Attaching a small rubber "keeper" on the sucker hook is another small detail used regularly by veterans. The strength and weight of a larger sucker eventually enlarges the hole in the soft cartilage lip area where the big hook is attached. If you don't use an additional keeper, the sucker will soon shake free of the hook. A keeper will also help prevent a muskie from tearing the sucker off the hook. A small piece of inner tube makes a good keeper, but some anglers prefer a small plastic worm. Still others like a strip of pork rind.

Few anglers are aware of the single-hook rig's true versatility. It works great in shallow water, through heavy cover, and is exceptional in deep water. Nearly any fishing situation can be covered well with a single-hook rig by incorporating a variety of additional terminal items and every once in a while, a few modifications. The standard single-hook rig works great in shallow to mid-depth ranges, but additional weight is sometimes essential when fishing deep water. Weighted sucker hooks are available commercially in a variety of sizes; however, since they're not a big selling item, they're often hard to find. If you aren't able to locate any, attach rubber-core sinkers of various weights to your wire leader or further up on your line, above the leader.

Large slip-sinkers are not recommended because muskies will usually swim around with a big sucker for quite some time before actually swallowing it. A slip-sinker complicates things because it allows the line to flow through while it rests on the bottom, increasing the amount of slack between you and the fish. This, in turn, reduces your ability to feel what is happening. Slip sinkers also increase the chances of your line becoming fouled on obstructions. A fixed sinker such as a rubber-core will be carried with the live bait after the strike, allowing it to stay in direct contact with the fish.

It's highly unlikely that a muskie will drop a sucker even with the additional weight. Big suckers commonly weigh between 1 and 3 pounds. A ½- to 1-ounce lead weight is relatively insignificant by comparison. The only thing that will spook a muskie into dropping a weighted rig is if it gets caught on an obstruction while the fish is moving. This is why many professionals prefer to attach any weight as close to the hook as possible. In this situation, weighted hooks are a big advantage.

The question of when to set the hook after a muskie has taken a big sucker on a single-hook rig has been the center of many arguments. Some of the old-time sucker fishermen simply smoked a complete cigarette after a strike and then set the hook. While this worked to a degree, little is learned by using this concept. Today's top trophy muskie hunters prefer to stay in close contact with the muskie after a strike and observe its movements. These movements will indicate whether or not the fish has indeed swallowed the sucker. Most professionals agree that a muskie classically goes through three stages after striking a sucker or any other large baitfish. First, it nearly always strikes the sucker sideways and continues to carry it in its mouth that way for awhile. This is called the "carry period," and it can last anywhere from two to 40 minutes. It's characterized by the muskie moving constantly in small circles with infrequent short pauses.

After swallowing a 24-inch sucker, this 27-pound muskie lost its battle. Anglers should always set the hook during the "swallow period" when fishing for muskies with suckers.

Eventually, the muskie will stop and begin actually swallowing its prize. This is commonly called the "eating period." It is not advisable to set the hook at this time since you can't be certain whether or not the fish has fully swallowed the sucker placing the hook in the right position. After swallowing the sucker, muskies usually take off in a quick burst, and continue moving at a more rapid pace than anytime before. And, instead of swimming in small circles, they will usually head out in one direction. Most of the time muskies that have swallowed a sucker will rise up off the bottom, too. Sometimes, they'll even boil on the surface or actually jump out of the water. All or any of these things indicates that the "swallow period" is at hand, and it's *hookset time*. Pick up all the slack, get fairly close to the fish, and slam the hook home as hard as possible.

Big Suckers—Fall Muskies

Cold-front muskies, in general, are more catchable on live-bait presentations. These fish are less apt to chase down a fast-moving lure. Yet, a lively sucker minnow dancing nervously close by is usually too much to resist. There is simply no lure that can match the authenticity of the "real thing." Suckers are a preferred natural forage that big muskies just love to sink their teeth into.

Working these lively suckers tightly to cover is a must. It should wiggle, bump, twitch or nudge things as much as possible. Sometimes, a large weedless hook is necessary so you can work the live sucker effectively around thick cover, without hanging up. However, big sucker hooks are not available in weedless models. But, they can be easily modified by rigging a short plastic grub or worm "Texas Style," the way bass fishermen do. It's also fairly easy to tie your own wire weed guard on these big squared hooks. A small piece of stainless steel wire no thicker than .0020 is best.

All sizes of suckers will take muskies, but the best size for lunkers is big suckers of 18 inches or more. Bigger suckers discourage smaller fish from striking and attract bigger fish which regularly feed on forage 15 inches and longer. It's not uncommon for a muskie that weighs in at over 30 pounds to grab a sucker that is more than 2 feet long!

The new quick-set rig is another popular setup when fishing suckers for fall muskies. The two or three hooks can be anchored in various portions of the minnow body for immediate hookset capability. Quick-set rigs are also a great asset if you plan on releasing the fish. Most muskies caught on quick-set rigs are not hooked deeply, so they can be released unharmed. Check out all the new quick-set items available from various manufacturers. New ideas are popping up almost daily. Quick-set rigs are recommended whenever big suckers are not available. In this situation, nearly any size muskie is apt to strike. Occasionally, big muskies are taken on smaller suckers, but more fish under 40 inches are likely to grab offerings in the 8- to 15-inch range. Small, single-hook rigs reduce the chances of mortality of fish caught on live bait.

Fishing efficiently with all of these sucker rigs requires a special device on a baitcasting reel commonly called a "bait clicker." This is a small feature on the side plate of most larger baitcasters that, when engaged, makes a loud audible clicking sound. After the line has been let out, and a sucker rig is in position, the free spool is left in the open mode while the bait clicker is engaged.

Baitcasting reels with "bait clickers" are essential for successfully using suckers when fishing for muskies. The pointer indicates the location of the clicker on this reel.

Using a quick-set rig in combination with the sucker hook provides added insurance that at least one hook will be in position when a muskie strikes. Note the "stopper" on the sucker hook to keep the sucker from pulling free.

This stops any further line flow from the reel unless the sucker is picked up by a fish or becomes snagged. At that point, the additional resistance will draw line off the reel, which in turn, sounds off the bait clicker. Obviously, this sound alerts the angler to check things out.

If the angler then determines that the resistance is nothing more than a snag, the rig can be freed and placed back in a rod holder. However, if the telltale strong tug or line burst indicates a strike, the clicker can be disengaged, and the angler moves to phase two which is setting the hook. With a single-hook version, however, it means it's time to follow the fish.

Shore-fishing suckers off a deep point in a big lake, or below a dam or major bend with a deep hole in a big river is a very popular method for late-fall muskies. This system is especially productive on those seemingly impossible days to fish because of the cold, howling winds and pelting rain or snow that tend to quickly dampen a fisherman's enthusiasm. However, a group of anglers can build a fire, put out a bunch of sucker rigs and effectively fish for lunkers. In this case, there are few alternatives. Inclement weather virtually eliminates any other form of presentation. Yet,

Complete Angler's Library

this kind of weather often stirs up some big-fish activity. It's simply a matter of being able to fish for them effectively. Shore-fishing may be the only way to salvage a fishing trip that is sabotaged by the adverse weather..

Fishing trophy muskies with big suckers will continue to be one of the best methods, especially in the fall. Elusive lunkers are more active during the fall, and nothing looks more tempting to their ravenous appetites and vicious teeth than a lively, wiggling, big sucker. If you don't mind fishing in cold weather, and know where some big muskies hang out in the fall, you just might be in for some unforgettable fishing.

=14=

Ice Fishing For Pike—Muskies, Too

Fishing through the ice for pike has really become its own sport during the last few years. Anglers all across Canada and the U. S. have learned that fishing for pike during the frozen water period can mean exciting fishing action. It wasn't too many years ago that only the hardiest fisherman pursued pike in the wintertime, but modern technology has changed that. With the advent of portable fish houses, lightweight heaters, power ice augers, depthfinders that shoot *through* the ice, fishing gear made specifically for ice fishing and clothing that really does keep an angler warm, the modern day ice angler is comfortable and mobile.

Today's ice anglers also have the advantage of national television shows, video tapes, seminars given by professionals and many fine magazines, including *North American Fisherman*, which detail successful ice-fishing techniques.

Jigging For Ice Pike With A Depthfinder

Taking a good-sized northern pike on a short jigging rod is one of the most thrilling forms of ice-pike angling. We are going to take a look at jigging techniques, jigging lures and equipment. When it comes to jigging for northern pike, one piece of equipment can make all the difference in the world to your angling success—the depthfinder.

When you are fishing from a boat, the first thing you probably do is switch on your depthfinder. A depthfinder is your underwa-

When you are after some good-sized ice pike, spending a little time with a depthfinder to determine the water depth before drilling a hole can save valuable time and energy.

Ice Fishing For Pike—Muskies, Too

ter eyes. It tells you how deep the water is, whether the bottom is hard or soft and if fish are present. There's a lot of valuable information obtained by merely turning on a switch. Preparing a depthfinder for ice fishing is easy. No. 1, it should be mounted in some type of box. The box should be light, compact and easy to carry, yet large enough to hold a 12-volt motorcycle battery. If you don't want to build your own depthfinder box, there are commercially-made ones available. A motorcycle battery is a good choice because without adequate power, a depthfinder is useless. The transducer should also be mounted on a swivel arm so that it can be swung up out of the way during transportation, and then easily swung down into the ice hole while fishing. It's also important to glue a bubble level to the top of the transducer to ensure that it is pointed straight down. Many anglers choose to use a narrow-degree transducer cone for ice fishing. They want a cone that only shows the area below the ice hole.

Using a depthfinder on the ice will save you time because you can read the water depth and structure through the ice before drilling a hole. If you have a topographical map of the lake and know the general location of a weedbed or offshore rock pile, you can use a depthfinder to locate the particular piece of structure. Simply pour a little liquid onto the ice and then set the transducer in it. It's just a matter of walking along and checking the water's depth through the ice until you find what you are looking for. Not only does a depthfinder save you time and energy, it makes you more mobile on the ice. It's important to be able to move quickly and easily while searching for fish or different types of fish-holding structure.

During the dead of winter, pike spend considerable time in deep-water haunts. You may find them on rock bars in depths of 20 to 40 feet. It's also not uncommon to locate pike suspended over deep water, say 30 feet down in 80 feet of water. Pike have been caught at 65 feet by anglers fishing for deep-water perch. Yet, fishing these areas would be hit-or-miss at best unless you use a depthfinder. A depthfinder lets you know if pike are present, and at what depth they are holding.

A huge advantage in using a depthfinder while ice fishing is that you not only see the fish, but your lure as well. This makes it easy to present your lure at the precise depth at which the fish are holding. There is no guess work. With this capability, the odds

Complete Angler's Library

Even after you've cut a hole, your depthfinder will be an effective monitoring device for a continual check on fish activity below the hole. Note that the depthfinder is fitted in a box for easy movement.

are tipped more in favor of the angler.

Once you are fishing at the right depth with fish present, it's a matter of presenting the right lure in a way that the fish find attractive. If you are jigging a flash spoon, for example, but are not catching any fish, you need to change lures, lure color, presentation speed or something else to draw a strike. If fish aren't showing up on the screen, you know it's time to move in trying to locate your prey. Depthfinders take a lot of the guess work out of ice fishing.

Equipment For Jigging

Pike are ferocious fighters, regardless of their size, and even a 4- or 5-pound pike will give you your money's worth of excitement. And, most of the time, a healthy 10- or 12-pound pike will put up more of a fight than a big pike. It takes stout equipment to

Ice Fishing For Pike—Muskies, Too   183 hold winter pike. The rod you use should have enough backbone to drive the hook home, yet enough flexibility to play the fish out. Both spinning and baitcasting reels will work, but many anglers prefer baitcasting with quality star drags. Line is very important. Some monofilaments become too stiff and brittle in cold weather; causing them to coil and break easily. Coiled line reduces the lure's action and makes setting the hook next to impossible. Dacron lines are another option. They won't coil; they stretch very little. However, they do soak up water and can freeze on your reel if you are fishing during extremely cold temperatures. This makes it impossible to give line to big fish.

Ten- to 15-pound line will be adequate, but don't forget to attach a wire leader. Pike's teeth are as sharp as high-priced shears, and they can cut the best of lines. Plastic-coated wire leaders aren't recommended because they cut down on a lure's action. Some anglers prefer to make their own leaders out of seven-strand wire. This proves to be advantageous in many situations.

Always use a quality ball-bearing swivel above the leader because some jigging lures can cause a terrific amount of line twist. You can attach the wire leader directly to the lure with a leader sleeve or use a pair of forceps to tie a knot. If you use forceps, run the wire leader through the eye of the lure twice, pull it up tight, leaving a 2-inch tail. Clamp the forceps onto the end of the 2-inch tail and grip the swivel in one hand and the lure in the other. Then, spin the forceps around the leader until the tail is completely wrapped around the leader. This process creates a knot that will not come loose and does not hinder the action of the lure—two important factors for success.

Uncoated seven-strand wire in 20- to 30-pound tests is smaller in diameter than most monofilament lines. It's flexible enough so that lure action is not hindered; yet, it prevents bite-offs.

It depends on the reason you are fishing for pike as to whether you use a gaff or not. More pike are lost in the ice hole than at any other time. A gaff will aid an angler in landing a pike, but a gaff can cause great bodily harm to the fish, making it impossible to release. If you are fishing for the table go ahead and use a gaff, but use it wisely. If you can see that the pike is too small to keep or is a trophy that you might want to release, land him with your hands. Don't injure a fish that you might decide to release.

Landing a pike by hand, even one weighing more than 20

These anglers opened a good-sized hole in the ice so they wouldn't have trouble bringing the pike up onto the ice. The result was a nice stringer of fish. The sled carries their equipment.

pounds is not that difficult. The most difficult part is getting a big pike started up through the hole. Once started, your troubles are pretty much over. The main thing is not to force it. Slowly raise it up toward the surface. Sometimes, it'll try a run at this point and come shooting part way out of the hole under its own power. Then, it's a matter of getting your fingers under a gill plate and lifting while maintaining tension on the line. Never try to lift it by the line alone.

Jigging Lures That Work

A multitude of good lures are available for jigging pike through the ice. The type, size and weight of the lure that you choose will depend on the depth of water that you will be fishing. If you are after deep-water pike you want a lure that is heavy enough to sink quickly and straighten the coils out of the line. If the lure is too light, it takes too long to drop into the depths so you lose contact with your lure. If you are jigging shallow bays, you can get by with lighter, smaller lures.

Lures such as large Rocker Minnows, CastMasters, Swedish Pimples, Jigging Rapala's, flash spoons and airplane jigs are all good bets for fooling an ice pike. Keep an assortment of weights, sizes and colors on hand. It sometimes helps to tip the lure with a live fathead minnow, minnow head or perch eye (where legal). It's also important to keep the hooks sharp. Sharp hooks mean more hooked fish.

Jigging In The Shallows

In addition to using a depthfinder to jig for deep-water pike, don't disregard the unit in shallow water. The depthfinder will help you locate weedlines and breaklines—good areas for locating winter pike. Pike seem to follow these breaklines, and the outside and inside edges of weedlines. A depthfinder will help you find these types of structure. Also, look for areas in the back of bays where weeds or other underwater structure form areas that funnel pike movement into narrow corridors through a bay. These kinds of spots are good to locate so you can set up an ambush point.

Many anglers don't realize that pike travel in schools. Schools of pike will move into a bay and go on a feeding frenzy. They act like a pack of wolves moving through an area, flushing out their prey. It's just a matter of the angler being in a good location and waiting for the action to begin. Pike will feed off and on during the day. First light is always a productive time, which is often followed by two or three hours of slow fishing before another feed. Early afternoon is usually quiet, but from 3 p.m. until dark the action is often good. Jigging for pike also works well with tip-up fishing. It helps an angler to stay active and occupied while waiting for a tip-up flag to fly skyward.

Jig Presentation

You don't have to be subtle when jigging for winter pike. If pike are aggressive enough to take a jig, they are on the attack. Often, they will scream out of nowhere and slam the jig as it free-falls. When this happens, they nearly rip the rod out of your hand. The strikes aren't always of a slam, bam, vicious nature, however.

Jigging, even with smaller, lighter lures, is productive when going after ice pike, as this young angler will attest. If you use a gaff, be sure to gaff the pike through the lower lip, as shown.

Sometimes, pike will move in on a jig, observe its action and then simply suck it in. This type of less-aggressive strike usually leaves the fisherman feeling a slight "thud" when the pike grabs the bait. Which means if you feel anything "different," set the hook and hang on. Jigging with a depthfinder will help you catch those less aggressive pike because you can use it to "customize your presentation" to the fish directly beneath your hole.

While jigging, it's best to always have the depthfinder on and watch the lure rise and fall on the screen. If a pike moves in to watch the lure, your depthfinder will show it. When you know that a pike is watching your lure, you can go into a more deliberate presentation. A pike that is in a nonaggressive mood really has to be enticed to strike. Lift the lure up slowly before letting it free fall and come to a rest. Then, give it a few light flicks, just enough to

Ice Fishing For Pike—Muskies, Too   187

make it quiver. Usually that will trigger the pike into striking. If there are still no strikes, jig the bait 6 or 8 inches up and down, then let it rest before barely twitching it again. If there's still no action, go to an aggressive jig. Lift the lure high and let it free-fall to a rest and then repeat the action. Keep rotating the jigging action until the pike hits or leaves. Remember that in almost all cases the pike will strike as the lure falls. Or, it will hit just at the end of the free fall.

Big Jigging Baits Aren't Always The Answer

Some anglers jig for bluegills, as well as pike. Iowa's Lake Okoboji is an excellent bluegill lake, and also the home of many northern pike. The lake is so clear that you can see down to 20 feet (if you're in a fish house), and observe the fish you catch. It means lots of opportunities to learn things.

For example, there are times when winter pike prefer small bluegill jigs over larger baits. The problem is they often come in so fast that there is no time to react. Generally, however, pike approach small bluegill jigs slowly, then gently pick them up. If the pike is small and you don't want to mess with him, quickly raise and hold the jig until the pike leaves. With bigger pike, it's fun to see if you can land them on the small jig and light line. Amazingly, a few can be landed, not many, but a few. Most of the time, the pike get into the weeds and bust off.

Recently, well-known angler Bob Jensen and Minnesota Twins first baseman Kent Hrbek were jigging for bluegills with small teardrops, 4-pound line and light jigging rods from inside a portable fish house. Hrbek was enjoying watching fish take his bait, but he wasn't expecting a big pike to swim in under his hole and pick off his jig. Kent set the hook, but the fish didn't move. It probably didn't realize it was hooked. So, Hrbek used a little more pressure, and the pike took off on a screaming run. Hrbek still managed to land the 16-pound, 9-ounce fish. (Quite a feat on light tackle!)

Tip-Up Tactics And Modifications That Catch Pike

All across the northern reaches of this country and Canada, tip-up flags popping skyward send ice anglers' hearts into overdrive. Nothing is guaranteed to wake an angler faster. And, not only is fishing for pike with tip-ups exciting, it works. Several ex-

Here, a polar tip-up is ready to be placed in a hole. Advantages to this type of tip-up include the low profile above the ice, and the submerged reel that prevents the line from freezing in the hole.

cellent tip-up models are marketed and some of them are quite sophisticated. Even so, there are ways that you can modify tip-ups to make them even better. Plus, there are little-known secrets that will help you put more pike on top of the ice. Here's a look at those tip-up tactics and modifications. Remember, it is usually the little things that add up to big fish.

Many types of tip-ups are sold in sporting goods stores and bait and tackle shops, and the price can range from $3 up to $20. The inexpensive models are nothing more than a couple of folding sticks placed across the ice hole to support an inexpensive plastic reel spool under water. They do have a triggering device that releases a spring-held flag when a strike occurs. These tip-ups do work, but they have some shortcomings, so you'll probably be happier with more expensive models.

Probably the most sophisticated and best-working tip-up on the market is the Polar. This tip-up is made from heavy-duty plastic, but is still compact and lightweight. It folds for ease in carrying; several of them will fit into a 5-gallon bucket. The Polar tip-up's reel sets under water and is attached to a spindle in a grease-filled tube which protects the spindle from freezing up. These tip-ups are also adjustable for tension, so that larger live baits won't trip the flag. If you are using small minnows for bait, reduce the tension so light strikes will trip the flag.

Most tip-ups are designed to present either live or dead bait in a suspended, horizontal position. If you want more bait movement, a Windlass tip-up holds the reel above the ice and has a rocking arm with a wind sail. It will actually jig your bait up and down, using the wind as its power source. All you have to do is adjust the spring tension for the amount of jigging action that you want. The only drawback to the Windlass is that the line starts from a reel above water so, in extreme cold, the line can freeze in the hole. This makes it impossible to jig or detect strikes.

Modification Of A Tip-Up

One of the biggest drawbacks to many tip-ups for use in fishing for pike is that their reel spools are too small to hold enough line. If you are any distance at all away from your tip-up, a hard-charging pike can strip all the line from the reel before you can reach the hole. That means lost fish.

The first thing you should do with a tip-up is exchange the small reel for a larger one. It only takes a few minutes to change the reel. The larger reel not only holds more line, but it allows the line to run more freely.

Choice of tip-up line is another important item. Your tip-up will function no better than the line that you use. Some anglers get by with monofilament line on their tip-ups, but it's not advisable. Most monofilament line gets stiff and coils in the cold. When this happens, the line is hard to keep on the reel. Line that coils and is brittle causes too many problems, even getting a good hookset is hard to achieve. However, several manufacturers now market special cold-weather monofilament line that is designed to stay more limber in cold water.

You see many fisherman with dacron line on their tip-ups. Dacron does have some good qualities; it doesn't coil, it flows freely

You can take pike like this on lighter, cold-weather lines, if you're prepared. However, you'll need more line so the pike can run; and, it should be limber enough to prevent kinks, coils and lost fish.

Ice Fishing For Pike—Muskies, Too

from the reel, has no stretch and remains strong. Dacron also has a couple of faults. When an angler handlines it while pulling in a fish, it has a tendency to tangle badly while piling up on the ice. It also soaks up water, so it can freeze to the ice while the angler is retrieving it. Dacron line has been known to tangle so badly from landing a pike that the reel had to be respooled with fresh line. However, there is one other good line choice for tip-ups: fly line. Fly line is strong, will not coil or soak up water, and stays soft and limp in cold weather. Fly line also flows off a spool easily.

One small, inexpensive piece of equipment that comes in handy when fishing tip-ups, is a common button. Take the fly line and thread it through one of the holes and back through another. It is a simple, yet effective, depth marker that is easy to use.

When you first put the tip-up out, you should always set it so the bait is suspended a couple of feet above the bottom. Most anglers use a clamp-on sinker to find the bottom, then they reel the line back up to where they want the bait suspended and set the tip-up in the hole.

Now the button comes into play. After determining the depth at which you want the bait suspended, slide the button up the line to where the line enters the reel. Then, when a strike occurs, you don't have to check the depth again when resetting the tip-up. It's just a matter of rebaiting, dropping the bait in the hole and reeling the line out to the button marker. This saves downtime.

Another problem with most tip-ups is that the strike-indication flag is too small to be seen from certain angles and during certain weather conditions. An angler can get spread out a bit when fishing in states like South Dakota which allow anglers to fish multiple tip-ups (four in South Dakota). Small tip-up flags can be hard to see from even short distances. In order to improve the visibility of tip-up flags, put a larger size on. Also, add a black flag along side the orange flag. On some days, depending on the cloud cover, brightness and angle of the sun, black shows up better than orange.

The size of the ice hole is also important. A 10-inch hole is a popular size. Big pike require some room to land and it's easier to get a big pike started up through a larger hole.

Tip-Up Placement

Tip-ups work either in deep or in shallow water. Most often

you find anglers fishing tip-ups in bays, off points, along weedlines or even over underwater humps. The key to tip-up placement is locating areas that you expect them to cruise into as they feed. You can also fish tip-ups out in deep-water areas where pike hold between feeding periods. But, you will have more success if you fish where the pike feed instead of where they rest.

When setting tip-ups in a bay, place them in strategic locations. Look for areas where pike will be funneled into narrow travel corridors, and areas where weed growth or breaklines act like fences and control pike movement. One avid ice pike angler refers to his tip-ups as a mine field. Basically, that's what it is. Tip-ups that are set in strategic ambush points will draw many more strikes then tip-ups placed at random.

Flooded areas are also good spots to intercept cruising pike. When fishing these areas, use the same technique as in a weedy bay. Remember that pike are drawn to the weeds and flooded timbered areas because baitfish are also drawn to these same areas. Baitfish use the weeds and timber to hide from the pike. Meanwhile, the pike use the weeds or timber as ambush points or they swim through trying to flush their prey into the open.

Don't be afraid to move the tip-ups. Some areas of a bay will attract large numbers of pike while other areas are barren. That means you should move if you're not catching any fish. Two hours is a good goal to set as a maximum amount of time fishing a particular hole without a bite. It works well to pull the tip-ups that were set first and leap frog over the others. Just keep drilling new holes out in front of the spread and keep leap frogging the tip-ups as you work across the bay or bay's shoreline. Keep this up until you locate an area that pike are working. Then, concentrate your efforts in that area.

Bait And Tip-Ups

Bait on tip-ups can vary from area to area. Northern pike will take a wide variety of either dead or live bait during the winter. If you're fishing with live bait, use baitfish that are indigenous to the area. This will increase your chances of success.

Three- to 4-inch bluegills are good bait wherever legal. Live creek chubs and suckers in the 6- to 8-inch range are also good pike baits. If there is a chance of catching a large pike, try suckers as large as one pound. Pike have a mouth and throat much like a snake which allows them to swallow huge baits, so don't be afraid to offer them.

Dead Bait In The Winter

Dead bait is an excellent winter and early-spring bait. It will catch lots of pike, especially big females that are starting to feel spawning urges. They know that ice-out and the spawn is just around the corner. Even though the big fish are on the move and in a feeding mood, their metabolism rate is low and they are not into chasing food for a meal. Dead bait is the answer. You will most likely catch more and bigger pike with dead bait than anything else. When it comes to dead bait nearly anything will work, but smelt, suckers and ciscoes lead the list. More pike are probably caught on smelt than any other dead bait, with dead suckers coming in a close second.

Most pike seem to prefer the dead bait hanging nose-down a couple of feet above the bottom. However, there have been times when laying the bait right on the bottom is effective. In fact, pike pluck chubs that have fallen from a jig off the bottom. It appears that pike may cruise solely for that purpose. Anglers have experimented by laying dead bait right on the bottom while fishing with a tip-up and found it to be an extremely productive way of catching last-ice pike.

Dead-Bait/Live-Bait Combination

Marlyn Ormseth, a bait and tackle shop owner at Sioux Falls, South Dakota, is an avid ice-pike angler who grew up chasing ice pike. Always looking for a better way of doing things, Marlyn experiments a great deal. Every once in awhile he comes up with a winning technique.

Marlyn developed a live-bait/dead-bait combination that really catches pike. In fact, the live-bait/dead-bait combination has caught pike when other baits have failed. Marlyn calls his rig the North View Special Pike Rig, after his bait and tackle shop. This quick-set rig consists of two No. 4 treble hooks and a No. 2 treble hook. All the hooks are held together with seven-strand wire. The main leader is about 14 inches long and attaches to the No. 2 treble hook. Over the shank of the No. 2 treble hook is a standard split ring. Another wire piece runs through the split ring. This 2-inch piece has a No. 4 treble on each end.

Dead bait is extremely effective when fishing for winter pike, as indicated by this angler's stringer. The combination of dead and live bait also works well because the dead bait supplies the smell and the live bait the action.

The dead bait used on this rig is usually frozen smelt. First, a nail is used to make a pathway through the center of the frozen smelt. The main leader is then inserted through the smelt and the No. 2 treble hook is embedded into the smelt's midsection. One of the No. 4 trebles is then hooked in the smelt's head while the second is hooked in the smelt's tail. Once the smelt is placed on the quick-set rig, live minnows are added. One large fathead minnow is tail-hooked to each No. 4 treble hook. The live minnows give this rig action while the smelt gives the rig odor. Pike just love the combination. More than 100 pike a day have been caught using Marlyn's dead-bait/live-bait rig.

Because this rig takes considerable time to set up, bait the rigs beforehand and keep them in a bait bucket. When there is a strike, the angler takes his bait bucket along. When the pike is

Ice Fishing For Pike—Muskies, Too

Results like this make it all worthwhile. Dead-bait/live-bait rigs are particularly potent in taking ice pike. Smelt is normally used for dead bait and minnows for live.

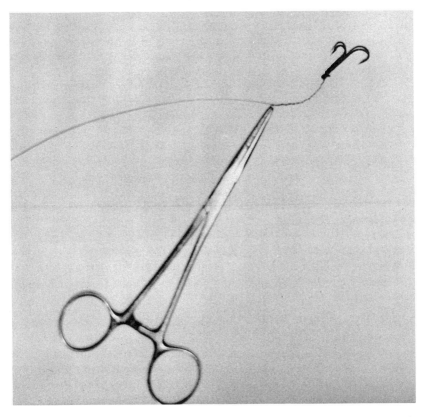

When going after winter muskies and pike through the ice, you'll need wire to prevent bite-offs. This shows a forceps attaching a hook directly to a wire leader.

landed, it's a simple matter to unsnap the hooked pike, leaving the hooks in its mouth, and then snap a baited rig on the line. This way, you're fishing again in seconds. This approach saves lots of downtime. And, the longer you keep your baited hook in the water, the better your chances are of catching more pike.

One word of caution when it comes to releasing wintertime pike: If it is cold, a pike's eyes can freeze in seconds, permanently damaging them. If the pike you catch is small, and you know that you are going to release him, do so in a hurry. It's not hard to unhook him in the water if you are wearing a pair of neoprene fishing gloves and using a jaw spreader. Your fingers even stay warm.

Quick-Set Rigs

Many say that a quick-set rig is the best hooking device for pike. Not only do they hook just about every fish that hits, they allow an angler to safely release the pike that he or she catches. Rarely does the fish have time to swallow the bait. Quick-set rigs are fast becoming the way to catch pike. Once an angler experiences the results obtained from quick-set rigs, he will always have them in his tackle box. They are that good—ask any angler, especilly pike and muskie anglers.

Muskies Through The Ice

When it comes to catching muskies through the ice, an angler really has his hands full. Muskies don't cooperate very well with ice anglers. There are always a few caught, but most are caught by accident or by true die-hard muskie fishermen.

Take the Iowa State record muskie that was caught during the winter of 1989. This beauty weighed nearly 40 pounds and was taken on a small CastMaster while the angler was fishing for deep-water perch and walleyes. Basically, it was an accidental catch, although you have to give the angler credit for wrestling such a monster up through a hole in the ice.

If a fisherman is serious about catching a muskie through the ice, he will probably experience his best success at first ice. Up to this time, muskies have not been pressured by anglers; therefore, they are still active. When looking for early-ice muskies try deep-water areas with hard bottoms first. Usually, you'll find first-ice muskies hanging around the same haunts that walleyes use. The first deep water off rocky points or deep rock piles are good places to check because this is where the walleye fishermen would be looking for walleyes. And, where there are walleyes, there is a good chance that muskies may be there, too.

These early-season muskies can be caught by using the same techniques used to take deep-water pike and walleyes. Tip-ups baited with large live bait work; so does jigging. Using large, live bait is the key to enticing muskies to bite.

As winter continues, the muskie fishing that wasn't fast to begin with really comes to a halt. Muskies just seem to hole-up and do nothing. Catching a muskie in mid- and late winter is next to impossible.

At ice-out, muskies, like pike, become more active, cruising shallow areas of the lake. It's not uncommon to see them in only 2 or 3 feet of water. In most areas, muskie season is closed during this time and anglers don't really get a chance to experience much late-ice muskie action. Panfishermen, from time to time, encounter late-ice muskies. However, these encounters are rare and are usually won by the muskie, anyway.

Most muskie fishermen would rather fish those big monsters during the open-water period. For whatever reason, they prefer to leave muskies alone during the winter months and test their skills in open water. Anglers who have caught muskies in the winter are a select few. They earn every one that they catch. These fish don't come quick or easy.

Muskies And Pike:
Conservation And Preservation

=====15=====

Caring For The Resource

Hunting for muskies or big pike is a real challenge. That's why so many people are hooked on fishing for them. It's a thrill just seeing these fish, let alone experiencing the wild strikes at the boat or battles that strain the strongest of equipment. Today's muskie and pike hunters are very good at what they do. They are well-read, well-equipped and they catch fish. Frankly, today's anglers are almost too good. That's why it's so important for all anglers to practice catch-and-release and follow fish and game laws. The fish and game departments in most states and provinces have instituted regulations to protect pike and muskies so that our children and grandchildren will enjoy good fishing.

Provinces, such as Manitoba, have gone as far as making barbless hooks mandatory. Many states and Canadian provinces have also started programs to educate anglers in proper catch-and-release tactics, and some even reward them for releasing big fish.

Does Catch-And-Release Work?

Catch-and-release, like anything else, has been a learning experience for today's angler. Trial and error is sometimes the best teacher. Thanks to the efforts of clubs like the NAFC, fish and game departments, fishing magazines and advice from the professionals, big pike and muskies are being successfully released. In fact, studies show that 90 percent of all muskies caught are being released alive. Many serious fishermen now carry their own fish

This angling couple doesn't have to be convinced that slot limits work. The larger Manitoban pike measured 50½ inches in length, and the smaller one weighed 18 pounds.

Caring For The Resource

tags and tagging devices. When fish are caught (this includes all fish species: muskie, pike, walleye or bass), they tag them, record the tag number, length of fish, time of catch and location. When the fish are caught again, more information is added to the records of that particular fish.

Successful recapture of muskies by ardent anglers in a number of protected waters reveals that catch-and-release works. Some have caught numerous tagged fish, and fish bearing hook scars. Incredibly, one angler has caught some of these fish more than once, including three weekends in a row. Interestingly, the fish (and others that were caught several times) come from the same location where they were caught previously.

Further proof that catch-and-release works comes from an Iowa Department of Natural Resources study. The purpose was to estimate survival and annual growth rates of male and female muskies in Spirit Lake. Muskellunge were first stocked in Spirit Lake in 1975 and the resulting fishery rapidly grew in popularity among Iowa's anglers. Fish captured as brood fish were tagged in the Spirit Lake hatchery after being measured and weighed, and then were released. Recapturing efforts were confined to examination of brood muskies captured and brought into the Spirit Lake hatchery. Tag numbers were recorded so that the year of tagging could be determined for survival estimates. The growth parameters of total length and weight were also noted for recaptures, providing annual growth information.

This survey showed that muskie survival rates in Spirit Lake ranged from .29 in 1981 to .80 in 1985. Some of this variability can be explained by the nature of the developing fishery and angler attitudes and utilization. Prior to 1981, the fishery was still expanding and fish were protected by a 30-inch minimum length limit. Also, muskie fishing was very limited. In 1981, the majority of tagged fish had grown into the 30- to 36-inch range. During that fishing season, the "Spirit Lake muskie rampage" occurred, and many of the fish were caught and kept.

Following this initial period, the muskie population shifted to larger sizes and there has been a definite trend toward catch-and-release angling. Muskie anglers are typically looking for that bigger-than-already-caught fish. Survival estimates which seemed low in 1981 have risen, possibly reflecting the catch-and-release trend. Survival estimates may decrease again because anglers are

As more catch-and-release situations develop, NAFC Members should be prepared to handle the fish with the best care. This includes procedures shown here, such as wearing protective gloves and trying to keep the fish in the water as much as possible.

starting to keep the good-sized muskies.

Survival records, which in part are estimates substantiated by facts, may not be 100 percent correct, but they do point to the fact that catch-and-release seems to work.

The provinces of Manitoba and Saskatchewan have been very instrumental in pointing the way to successful fishery management. Both provinces have experienced a decline in the number of trophy pike in many of their lakes, especially in their northern-most areas. The problem began years ago when anglers would fly into remote lakes containing an abundance of large northern pike (where they would sort and keep the largest fish to fill their possession limits). No slot or length limits were in place at that time to protect the fish.

It was soon discovered that heavy fishing pressure could destroy the trophy pike fisheries in these northernmost lakes because of their short growing period. It took a few years to catch most of the big fish, and as soon as they were gone, anglers simply moved on, leaving behind a poor fishery and an outfitter unable to entice anglers back to his place of business.

Manitoba recognized that something had to be done to preserve the quality of its resources, so it instituted slot limits. Daily and possession limits of fish were also reduced to protect existing fisheries. Have the regulations helped? Consider Lake Vandekerckhove. Located near the end of the road, north of the town of Lynn Lake, the lake is above the 57th parallel, about as far northwest of Winnipeg as you can drive in the province. Remote, yet still accessible, Lake Vandekerckhove was noted for its abundance of large pike, but the lake could not keep producing big pike as fast as anglers were removing them.

Several years ago, daily and possession limits were lowered on the lake, and any pike between the lengths of 30 and 41 inches had to be released. One trophy fish of over 41 inches could be kept, while anglers ate the remaining fish for shorelunch or took them home if they were under 30 inches. Manitoba also required anglers to use barbless hooks.

Big-fish-award programs were instituted to further encourage anglers to release large fish. Conversion factors (length and girth computed into pounds) were made available with emphasis on recording the *length* of the catch, not the weight. The less a big fish is handled, the better its chances of surviving after being released. Now anglers can simply measure their catch while it rests in the water and maybe hold it up for a quick photo. Then, release it. For their efforts, anglers receive special recognition with a certificate, pins and their names listed in the catch-and-release records.

Since Manitoba's laws were changed, Lake Vadekerckhove has once again grown into a quality pike fishery. In fact, recently, the biggest problem encountered there is catching pike *small enough* to keep. One pike recently caught there measured an incredible 50½ inches! Most anglers seem to be happy with the prospect of being able to catch large fish, even if they have to let them go. The days of fishing for meat are over.

Release Methods That Work
Successful methods of releasing fish have been learned

through trial and error. When fishermen first started releasing fish, most fish were netted, lifted into the boat, and the hook was removed from their jaw. Then, it was usually measured, maybe even weighed and then held up for photos. After all of this, the fish was returned to the water.

Anglers soon learned that landing nets can do more harm than good. Hooks catch in the webbing as fish struggle, often resulting in terrible tangles. This made the fish difficult to remove, and, at the same time, would remove the fish's scales and protective slime. The end result was stressed fish, ones that usually died after being released.

To prevent this, some thoughtful angler started using a cradle. A cradle is simply a couple of 1- by 2-inch boards about 5 feet long with about 3 feet of netting attached to them. When a pike or muskie is played out, it is brought to the boatside where the cradle is slipped under it. The cradle allows the fish to be left in the water while the hooks are being removed. Then, the fish can be held up for a quick photo before being placed back in the cradle until it has recovered. Once the fish looks and acts healthy, it is released.

Although this release procedure is much better than a landing net, it still is not the total answer. Some of these fish still die.

The more experienced a person gets at handling large fish, the easier it is to release large fish, like pike or muskies, alive. Most muskie professionals rarely net their fish. Instead, they prefer to remove the hook while the fish is still in the water.

In many cases, once a fish is played out, it is so tired that you can put your reel in free spool, set your rod down and grab the line. If the fish takes off, just control it with the line, bringing it back hand over hand. Get it along side the boat, steady the fish by grabbing it around the tail (or if it is small, across the back). Then, use your free hand and a "hook-out" to work the hooks free from its mouth.

Hook-outs are really tremendous tools because their offset handles give anglers greater leverage. If the fish thrashes, you can let go of your grip. Many people use regular or needle-nose pliers, but they're not nearly as good. The hook-out is better than anything else that you can use. It has strong jaws with which an angler can grab the hook and easily twist it free. Jaw spreaders are also not a bad idea. If a fish is hooked with a bucktail, for example, chances are good that the lure will be deep in the mouth. The

To reduce possible harm to this good-sized muskie, this angler won't bring the fish out of the water. While supporting the fish with one hand, he uses a hook-out tool to remove the lure.

spreader will hold the fish's mouth open while you reach in and remove the hooks.

Fish will usually lie rather quietly in the water while you are working on them. If the hooks are set extremely deep or the fish is caught by two or three trebles, a bolt cutter is the answer. A good model is about 7 or 8 inches long, and small enough to be handled with one hand. It's a great device for snipping hooks.

Ideally, fish should not be brought in the boat because the odds of them thrashing around and injuring themselves are too great. The fish will be much better off left in the water. If you do remove the fish from the water for photos, do not pick it up by the gill plates. It makes no sense to hang a 20- or 30-pound fish by its gill cover and expect that its weight will not damage its internal organs. If you are going to lift a fish up for a picture, lift it up horizontally and take a quick picture over the water. Don't lift it up vertically.

There are a couple of ways to measure fish while they're in the water. Mark various lengths on a canoe paddle that you can lay in the water next to the fish or put similar marks on the side of your boat. It's just a matter of pulling the fish up alongside for a measurement. You can use a cloth measuring tape to measure the fish's girth, if desired. You can, however, estimate its weight within a pound or two without it.

With today's modern taxidermy practices, a large fish does not have to be kept for mounting. In the next chapter, NAFC Members will learn more about this, plus tips on preserving your catch if you prefer to have your fish mounted.

=16=

Preserving Your Trophy

Good taxidermists are real miracle workers. Fish are often brought to them in ridiculously poor condition. Everything from torn fins to gaff wounds are common sights. These fish are brought to taxidermists by anglers fully expecting the end product to look like the display samples in the taxidermist's showroom. Little do they realize that while a lot of scars and torn fins can be repaired, the fish is sure to turn out far better if it is cared for properly right after being caught.

Of course, none of this matters if you choose to have a graphite reproduction of your fish. It is encouraged that you consider one because you can release your fish unharmed. Many anglers, however, prefer skin mounts of the actual fish. If you're one of them, here is how to make sure your next trophy mount lives up to your expectations.

Prepare Before You Go

Most people simply don't take fish appearance into consideration when fighting a trophy pike or muskie. That's understandable, considering the excitement of catching a trophy fish. But, the procedures you use for landing such a fish can have an enormous impact on the final mount. Gaffs, for example, leave a big puncture wound in the fish, and landing nets can be even worse because they can pull back a fish's scales, strip off most of its protective body slime, damage the eyes and destroy the fish's beautiful web-like fins, as well as the tail.

Leaving the net in the water after landing a fish reduces the fish's injury potential. The fish can still move around in the water, and it is less apt to get tangled in the net.

Preserving Your Trophy

Pike and muskies are exceptionally tough fish to keep in good condition for mounting because they're so big and powerful. Their typical thrashing and rolling antics inside a landing net makes for one big mess. Even a hand-landed pike or muskie can suddenly break loose, fall onto the boat's floor and self-destruct. In the process, tackle boxes get knocked around, loose lures often get lodged in the fish's body, and any sand or gravel on a boat's floor strip off its protective slime.

A recent incident in Vilas County, Wisconsin, is a worst-case scenario of what can happen. A successful angler was holding a 38-inch muskie horizontally for a quick photo before releasing it. The fish, however, suddenly flipped itself out of the angler's grasp. Its landing pad turned out to be the center of a styrofoam cooler filled with muskie lures! The muskie continued its wild thrashing, burying one hook after another into its sleek sides. By the time it was all over, the fish was in such bad shape that it had to be killed. Mounting it was also out of the question because it was so torn up; a disappointing ending to an otherwise jubilant moment.

With disastrous results such as this in mind, let's take a look at a few preparatory things to consider so that once a trophy is caught, it arrives at your taxidermist in the best shape possible. There are several things to consider, including the landing method; containment of the fish (livewell, cooler, garbage bag, burlap sack, etc.); and restoration photos. Following a few simple rules will insure that your trophy ends up at the taxidermist in its best possible condition.

Landing big pike and muskies is tricky—and dangerous—business. Both fish have huge, sharp teeth, and more than likely they have a big, multi-hooked lure hanging from their jaws. So, hand-landing, while it is less destructive to the fish overall, can be extremely dangerous. Heavyweight rubber or leather gloves should be worn.

Long-sleeve plumber's gloves are the best choice overall. They do not stiffen when dried like leather gloves do, nor do they retain fish slime or odor. The long-sleeve versions protect the wrist and lower arm area from hook penetration, as well. Everyone who fishes regularly for pike or muskies should carry along a set of these gloves for landing and photo purposes. Not only will they protect your hands from tooth and hook punctures, they will not damage the fish's protective slime or skin.

Heavyweight plumbers' gloves are ideal for handling large pike and muskies for disengaging the hook and for photographic purposes before releasing the fish. The gloves prevent injury to the angler and the fish.

Plumber's gloves can be found at any large hardware supplier, as well as many of the discount stores. They're often used not only for plumbing, but gardening and other outside work. These same gloves also work great for fish cleaning.

As grotesque as the subject of gaffing a pike or muskie sounds, "lip gaffing" does little damage and enables the angler to easily remove the hooks. Once the fish is at boatside, a small gaff hook is slowly inserted into the lower lip portion of the fish just in front of the tongue area. The fish is not lifted out of the water, but instead, the angler reaches out with a long-nose pliers or hook-out tool and disengages the attached hooks. If the fish is to be released, the gaff hook can be slipped out at this point, and the fish swims away without ever being lifted from the water. If the decision is made to keep the fish for mounting, it can be quickly lifted

Preserving Your Trophy

up and into a containment area such as a large livewell.

This lip-gaffing system is one of the best ways to handle a trophy to be mounted. The fins are never touched, body slime is never removed, and body scars from additional handling are avoided. Surprisingly, very few anglers use the lip-gaffing system. The gaff carries such a "kill" reputation from its use in saltwater that few pike and muskie anglers today even carry one onboard. Yet, when it's used in the manner described above, there is absolutely no "kill" involved.

There are ways when using a landing net to minimize damage to fins, slime and vital organs. First off, do not use a small net. Forcing a large pike or muskie to curl up into a small net with a short bag compounds the eye, organ, slime and fin damage referred to earlier. Big-hooped nets with deep bags simply give the fish more room inside with less overall stress.

Never lift a big pike or muskie out of the water right after it is netted. As soon as the fish feels and sees the net encircling it, it is sure to begin thrashing. This is when most fish are injured by the mesh, especially if the angler lifts it out of the water at this crucial time. It is much better to simply hold the net rim about a foot or so above the surface of the water and let the fish swim around inside. The water helps prevent fish injury by allowing the net to flex during the fish's movements, absorbing most of the blows.

When it's time to lift the fish out of a net, do so when the fish and the net are still in the water. Always avoid lifting the fish into the boat while it's still in the net. The fish is sure to thrash once again as soon as the net is lifted up, and will continue its violent argument as soon as the net bag hits the boat floor. A solid grip in the gill-plate area with plumber's gloves will help insure a damage-free lift.

Photos are best taken right after the fish is caught, too. Photos of dead fish taken later are just that—dead fish photos. Photos of a freshly caught trophy not only capture the best color of the fish, but the angler's jubilance, as well. Make certain cameras are not tucked away in the bottom of a hard-to-get-at storage area. The photographer should be shooting from the moment the fish is landed to the time it is placed inside a livewell. Photos sequenced from this moment on are sure to capture some great expressions and poses.

Mounting an 8-by-10 photo instead of the fish is growing in-

You've landed your trophy, removed it from the net without injury and taken its photograph. Now, it's decision time. Should you release or keep it? Photos can be used to make a replica while the fish lives to challenge another angler. This helps make the decision easier.

creasingly popular. So much emphasis has been placed lately on catch-and-release fishing that fewer anglers are keeping even their largest trophy pike and muskies. On top of that, many areas in Canada are now total catch-and-release fisheries which simply don't allow fish to be kept. The only "mount" you're going to get from such waters is either a photo or a replica. Getting a series of high-quality photos of your trophy from such fishing spots is important. The very best print film for enlargements of an angler posing with a big fish is one with an ASA rating of 100 or possibly 200. High film speeds are rarely needed for this kind of photography because most shots are taken in bright daylight.

Proper containment of your trophy, once boated, is essential. Most of the better boats sold today have livewells in the 48-inch range. These are ideal for protecting a trophy from any damage. If you are fortunate enough to own such a rig, it is advisable to place the trophy in the water-filled livewell right after the landing and photos, and head for the taxidermist. This insures a near-perfect fish for mounting. If the fish is caught late in the evening after all taxidermy shops are closed, icing down the trophy inside the livewell overnight is an acceptable alternative.

If the boat from which you are fishing is not outfitted with a livewell, subdue the trophy as soon as possible with a small club, cracking the fish right behind the eyes. This eliminates any further thrashing and consequently any cosmetic damage. Then, place the fish immediately inside a large, heavyweight garbage bag, and head for the taxidermist. If it's a late-evening catch, ice down the fish inside the bag, making sure to protect the tail from drying out.

Anglers fishing in remote areas should get the trophy into a freezer after it is enclosed in a garbage bag. Wrapping a folded piece of cardboard around the tail and taping it in place is good insurance against damage during freezing and transportation.

The type of paper, plastic or cloth used to wrap a trophy fish for freezing is very important. Certain paper products are bad, especially newsprint. A newspaper's ink can bleed onto fish leaving permanent marks. Clean, print-free paper is recommended. Just about any kind of large plastic bag works well, but some cloth products contain inks and oils, or other chemicals you should avoid. A large, white, terry-cloth beach towel works very well for wrapping a trophy. In fact, it is probably the best thing to use,

The best trophy preservation method is to photograph the fish and release it. Beautiful, graphite replicas can now be made from photographs. This taxidermist is putting the finishing touches on this muskie replica with an air brush.

especially if you wet the towel first before wrapping and freezing the fish.

When the fishing spot is a remote fly-in camp with no freezing facilities, preservation can be difficult. Keeping the fish alive on a stringer or in a homemade pen is one option, but quite often turtles, gulls, mink or other animals will destroy your fish before you leave. Icing it down is a consideration only if enough ice is on hand, and there's a large enough container available. Some fly-in fishermen have gone as far as taking in their own homemade wire live baskets for such a purpose, but most often such features simply don't exist. This is definitely a situation where good photos are a must. The best thing to do is photograph your trophy, then release it.

Above all, it is never advisable to skin-out a fish you want mounted, unless you have been personally instructed by a taxidermist on the proper procedures. Once you've taken a knife to a trophy, some irreparable damage is sure to occur. However, if skinning-out a trophy pike or muskie is the only way to get it out of a remote area, consult your favorite taxidermist for some instructions on the proper techniques.

Video cameras have really added a whole new dimension to capturing a once-in-a-lifetime trophy. New models will stand up to a surprising amount of abuse and can be hauled into virtually any remote location. As long as extra batteries and film are on hand, you can record the battle, weigh-in and release of a trophy on tape. Years later, the actual event, as it really happened, can be replayed over and over again.

Selecting a good taxidermist is the final, but most important decision. This is where most first-time trophy catchers make their biggest mistake. Too often, anglers base their decision on price alone. Usually, you get what you pay for. The very best taxidermists in the business take their time, use top-quality materials and have enormous pride in their work.

There are a few easy guidelines to follow when choosing a taxidermist. The first rule is go to a taxidermist with a known reputation. Professional guides and outfitters are usually good sources of information. They usually have a list of satisfied customers ready to brag about what a great job "so and so" did on their fish. If this option isn't available, go through the telephone book's advertising pages and call a number of taxidermists. Compare rates, and then compare their work.

The second rule is to go to a taxidermist who specializes in pike and muskie mounts. Think about it. A taxidermist who mounts mostly largemouth bass is less likely to do a pike or muskie correctly. You're better off making sure the taxidermist you choose mounts lots of pike and muskies. He knows the taxonomy and features of pike and muskie far better than a bass specialist.

Lastly, view samples of the taxidermist's work personally. If a friend brags about his mounted fish, take the time to go over to his office or home and check it out. If possible, view other mounts done by the taxidermist. Funny as it may seem, what looks like good taxidermy work to one person, might not be that impressive to another. Everyone has individual tastes in art, and taxidermy is a form of art.

The best taxidermists are excellent painters. Giving your taxidermist several photos of your trophy to use as references when painting time comes can really improve the final product. Top taxidermists who really care about their customer's needs prefer to have a photo from which to work. It simply makes the mount appear to be closer to the real thing. They are also sculptors. They can restore the body to a lifelike form, shape it in a pose that's exciting and paint it to look as though it is alive.

Surprisingly, some taxidermists have a difficult time painting both muskies and pike equally well. Some do a much better job on pike, but fall short on muskies, and vice versa. This is why personally seeing samples of a taxidermist's work is so important. Once you're totally confident with his or her abilities, have your fish mounted.

17

Future Looks Bright

Today's anglers have certainly come a long way in recent years in terms of fishing knowledge and capability. They are well read, well educated, well equipped and good at what they do. That leads to a new problem. We have become so proficient at catching fish that if we don't practice catch-and-release, it won't be long before we will fish the resource out. Enough of the scare tactics. The attitudes of most of today's anglers are changing. The days of filling the freezer with fish are fast becoming a thing of the past. Now, it's more important, at least to *most* anglers, to maintain a good fishery so the thrill of catching a trophy fish can be experienced over and over again. Unfortunately, there are some anglers who still think only of themselves. They want to keep what they catch, and, in a lot of cases, more than the legal limit. These types of anglers have been dubbed "Double Dippers," "Law Breakers," "Fish Hogs" and so on. Fortunately, the number of these people are on the decline as more and more anglers realize that the resource has to be protected and used wisely.

Hopefully, we'll never see the day when we cannot go out fishing and keep part of what we catch. Eating fish is part of fishing. There just isn't anything better than a shorelunch of fresh fish cooked over an open fire, or enjoying a few fish meals after returning home. Fish are great eating, and good for you.

But there are plenty of fish species out there such as crappies, bluegill and perch that make excellent tablefare, but will never

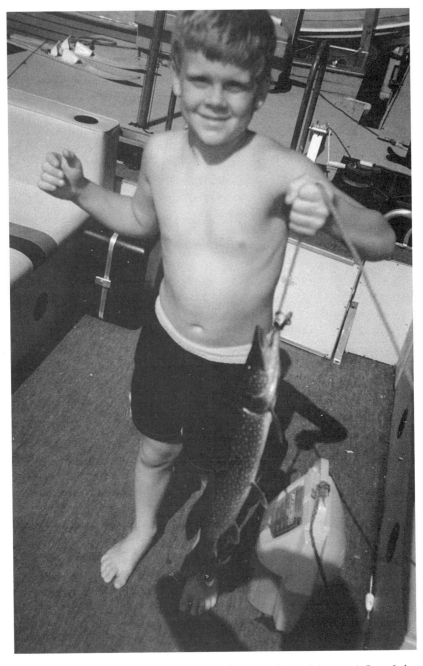

This proud 9-year-old caught his first northern pike in Pine City's (Minnesota) Cross Lake. Because of the growing concern for conserving this natural resource, his future looks bright for taking plenty of fish like this.

Future Looks Bright

offer the thrill of catching a trophy-sized fish. Knowing that makes it easier to turn pike and muskies back into the water to fight another day. Big pike and muskies are limited resources that require intense management if they are to survive. Even though most serious pike and muskie hunters are releasing the vast majority of the fish they catch, more time and effort has to be put into stocking and management programs. The future looks bright for at least some numbers of fish. However, it isn't so bright for big fish because too many big pike and muskies are being kept.

Here is a look at what some fish and game offices, Canadian provinces and privately funded fishing clubs, and leading fishing magazines such as the NAFC's official club publication, *North American Fisherman* are doing. The main effort of these organizations is to provide a solid fishery for the present and the future. It is also the aim of these organizations to educate the public in the importance of catch-and-release practices. Without the cooperation and participation of fishermen, the programs will fail. With everyone pulling together, we can all experience some fantastic trophy fishing, and have some fish for the table—all without hurting the resource.

Looking At Manitoba, Canada

Manitoba is at the geographic center of North America and its borders extend as far north as the seacoast of Hudson Bay, and as far south as the Minnesota and North Dakota borders. It's a vast vacation land of 250,000 square miles, three-fifths of which consists of verdant forest and crystal-clear waters pure enough to drink. The waters in Manitoba provide refuge for a diverse assortment of fish. In order to preserve or increase the quality of the fishery, Manitoba has implemented several programs. In 1958, for example, Manitoba introduced its Master Angler Awards program. Award certificates and badges were initiated in 1960. This program has been specially designed to give anglers recognition for their outstanding catches. In order to qualify, an angler must catch (with rod and line) any one of 28 fish species of a certain minimum size. In 1960, with only seven species of fish eligible for awards, 480 entries were processed. In 1990, when 28 species were recognized, the number of entries grew to an incredible 5,000.

On-going developments ensure continued growth in the program while maintaining viability and addressing conservation

Manitoba, Canada, has some of nature's best scenic elements. It has recently implemented minimum and maximum size limits, as well as slot limits, so that present and future fishing generations will be able to enjoy trophy pike fishing in the province's pristine lakes and rivers.

Future Looks Bright

concerns. The Department of Natural Resources and Travel Manitoba have encouraged communication and development of the program and have been rewarded with increased catch-and-release participation.

Anglers now submit applications listing only a fish's length, not its weight. This measure was instituted to aid anglers in practicing catch-and-release fishing. Fishermen who do release trophy fish are given special recognition through the Master Angler Awards program. The results of the program speak for themselves. The number of fish released has increased steadily from 42 percent in 1975 to 48 percent in 1980. That figure continues to grow. In fact, over 50 percent of all trophy fish registered in the Master Angler Awards program are now being released.

Size Limits For Fish In Manitoba

Minimum-size limits, maximum-size limits and slot limits—someone who enjoys fishing has probably heard of these terms. But, what do they mean? Why and where are they used?

Minimum-size limits mean all fish smaller than the specified length limit must be returned to the water. Minimum-size limits are often placed on waters with little or no natural reproduction and are periodically stocked to improve fish populations. These waters experience heavy fishing pressure. Minimum-size limits can also reduce the total annual harvest from a lake, while still giving anglers a chance to enjoy catching fish. The majority of lakes in the United States are heavily fished, yet all lakes can only produce a certain amount of fish every year. If anglers return small fish, fewer pounds are harvested by each angler. This results in more fish remaining in the lake for the next angler to catch.

Minimum-size limits are not effective on lightly fished lakes, or on productive lakes where the reproductive capacity of the fish population is high. Using a minimum-size limit in those cases can result in a large population of small fish just below the size limit, and virtually no "keepable" fish. Minimum-size limits are an effective way of reducing the harvest in heavily fished lakes, while at the same time allowing anglers to catch more fish.

Maximum-size limits allow the harvest of only one fish over the specified size limit. For example, on a lake with a maximum size limit of 30 inches, anglers can keep only one northern pike (or muskie or whatever species the law specifically mentions) that

What's the size? In many lakes in Canada, fish like this one must meet certain size requirements. Some also are strictly catch-and-release waters.

Future Looks Bright

length or longer. Any additional pike caught over that size limit must be returned to the water. Large fish are scarce and highly prized by anglers. These fish take many years to reach the maximum-size limit. Many trophy-sized fish are 20 to 30 years old.

The purpose of the maximum-size limit is to give more anglers the thrill of catching a large fish, and to distribute the trophies among more fishermen. The intermediate- to large-sized fish that are conserved this way are usually the most productive spawners, so the maximum-size limit serves a dual purpose. It maintains breeding stock, and provides more opportunities for trophy fish to be caught.

Instituting maximum-size limits is a relatively new idea. It's so new that studies have not shown the long-term impact on trophy fish populations. The idea, however, appears to show enough promise because several provinces and states have put it into use.

Slot limits require anglers to release all fish between certain lengths. For example, a lake that has a 30- to 41-inch slot limit means all pike longer then 30 inches and shorter than 41 must be released.

Slot limits allow anglers to take home small to intermediate-sized fish to eat, but protect the medium-sized fish in the slot so they can grow to trophy size. Slot limits also protect the majority of spawners. Slot limits are useful on waters that are capable of producing trophy fish. However, heavy angling pressure severely limits the number of fish that reach trophy size. Slot limits also help to sustain good fishing by both providing more spawners and reducing harvest, therefore increasing catch rates.

Iowa's Muskellunge Goals And Objectives

Angler interest in muskellunge fisheries created the atmosphere for the Iowa Conservation Commission, now the Iowa Department of Natural Resources, to investigate the concept of the introduction of muskellunge into Iowa waters. The program was initiated in 1960 when 40 muskie fingerlings were stocked in Clear Lake and a similar number went into West Okoboji. These fish were obtained as fry from Wisconsin and were reared at the Decorah, Iowa, hatchery until they reached 7 to 12 inches in length.

During the 1970s, the muskellunge stocking program was expanded to additional lakes. Lake Rathburn was stocked in 1970

The Iowa Department of Natural Resources initiated its muskellunge stocking program in 1960 with muskie fry like these. Although these programs have their supporters and critics, the stocking of muskies and hybrids has expanded the muskie range and anglers' enjoyment, as well.

and 1971; Big Creek Lake in 1976 and 1978; and Spirit Lake was initially stocked in 1975. Prior to 1975, stocking varied from a few fish to a few thousand fish for both Okoboji lakes and Clear Lake. The development of a reliable brood stock source, coupled with recent advances in artificial feeding techniques, has provided a dependable supply of muskellunge fingerlings to satisfy current fish-management requests.

Special-interest groups have voiced their support of the muskellunge program, but there are anglers who strongly oppose stocking muskies. These individuals have used the muskie as an easy scapegoat for the fluctuations experienced in the walleye and yellow perch fisheries the past several years. Yellow perch are the primary forage fish species found in these lakes. They are also a very popular sportfish species (ranking No. 1 in 1985 and 1986 and No. 3 in 1987, according to a Spirit Lake creel survey). The conflict between these user groups intensifies during years when weak-year classes of yellow perch move through the fishery.

Management has focused on the establishment and maintenance of a muskellunge fishery that is capable of providing Spirit, Clear and the Okoboji lakes' anglers a unique opportunity to fish for trophy muskellunge. The term *trophy*, when used to describe fish, conjures up many different impressions and values to various anglers, but usually means something to "show off." The state defines muskies of 40 inches or 15 pounds as trophies and anglers catching such fish qualify for the "Big Fish" award. This standard (40 to 45 inches, or 15 to 20 pounds) qualifies anglers for awards, and is common in the various states with muskellunge programs.

Regulations

Iowa's regulations (a daily limit of one fish with a minimum size of 30 inches) are intended to enhance the trophy-fishery philosophy and protect brood stock muskellunge. A survey of 16 states and four Canadian provinces revealed 13 states and one Canadian province had a one-fish daily limit with 30-inch minimum length, and six states and two Canadian provinces had special regulations with increased daily limits, usually two, and/or larger, minimum size limits, ranging from 32 to 40 inches.

Sportsmen Uniting For Better Fishing

NAFC Members and other anglers must realize that the future of fishing in North America, or anywhere else for that matter, will not be bright unless resources are pooled in making the story known to the individual states' legislatures and departments of natural resources. It's only through a joint effort that better fisheries and fishing's future can be insured for ourselves and our children's use.

Fishermen in Iowa have moved in that direction, forming Iowans for Better Fisheries (IBF). The IBF was formed to improve and protect the state's fishing waters. With the slogan "Today, Tomorrow ... for Ourselves, Our Children," this all-volunteer group of concerned Iowa anglers has started a membership drive to bring at least 20,000 of its fellow enthusiasts into a powerful organization that can serve as watchdogs for state, county and local legislation; push for beneficial projects and legislation; provide a statewide network of concerned anglers to quickly and powerfully deal with relevant issues; work with the Iowa DNR and other agencies, and keep its members informed and updated.

According to IBF's founder and board chairman, Marty Lamberti, legislators have long thought that Iowa's nglers are one of the least vocal groups in the state. That's sadly ironic, considering it is potentially one of the strongest, with over 250,000 fishing licenses sold each year.

"If the IBF's goal of 20,000 members is reached," says Jim Mayhew, Iowa's DNR Chief of Fisheries, "it could be the best thing to happen to Iowa's fishing since the formation of the Conservation Commission in 1936. The DNR hopes that IBF evolves into a strong statewide alliance." Already supporting the IBF are a number of bass clubs and fishing groups, along with individual members. Support is also being sought from Iowa corporations. Anglers in other states are taking similar steps. Many sportsmen's clubs across the country have been formed with the same goals in mind—to improve the fisheries and the environment.

The Future

Looking ahead, it's easy to see a bright future for muskie and northern pike fishing in North America. Anglers are becoming better educated in conservation practices, more folks in general are helping clean up our lakes, rivers and streams, and there seems to be a commitment being made to improve and expand the fisheries we have.

Index